Pittsburgh

that stays within you

by

Samuel Hazo

art by

Robert Qualters

Fourth Edition. Revised and enlarged.

The Local History Company
publishers of history and heritage

Pittsburgh, Pennsylvania, USA

The Pittsburgh that stays within you:
Fourth Edition. Revised and enlarged.
Copyright © 2004 by Samuel Hazo
Art by Robert Qualters

Published by
The Local History Company
112 North Woodland Road
Pittsburgh, PA 15232
www.TheLocalHistoryCompany.com
info@TheLocalHistoryCompany.com

The name "The Local History Company", "Publishers of History and Heritage", and its logo are trademarks of The Local History Company.

Back cover portait of Robert Qualters by Robert Qualters and Mark Perrott.
Front cover painting Panther Hollow Bridge by Robert Qualters, 1990.

Library of Congress Cataloging-in-Publication Data

Hazo, Samuel John.
    The Pittsburgh that stays within you / by Samuel Hazo ; art by Robert Qualters.—4th ed.
        p.   cm.
    ISBN 0-9744715-0-X (pbk.: alk paper)
    1. Hazo, Samuel John—Homes and haunts—Pennsylvania—Pittsburgh. 2. Poets, American—20th century—Biography. 3. Pittsburgh (Pa.)—Social life and customs. I. Title.

PS3515.A9877Z465 2004
811'.54—dc22
                                2003020585

Printed in USA

P R E F A C E

In memory of Anna Abdou

This is the fourth edition of a book that was originally published in 1986. In a forward to the first edition I wrote the following:

"A city-dweller named Aristotle remarked that a story should have a beginning, middle and an end. My memoir of Pittsburgh lacks a beginning and an end, but it assuredly has a middle. Commencing, as Aristotle would have approved, in the midst of things, it manages to stay right there. Since its unity is the unity of a single point of view entwined with anecdotes gathered haphazardly by the simple principle of addition, it could be extended from either end, and some day I may do just that if only to compensate for the numerous omissions that will be pointed out to me the moment this book is published. But for now it is what it is—a memoir that attempts to suggest that Pittsburgh did not arrive at its present status like Venus on the half shell, but that its present grew out of its past. That past exists in our collective memory if it exists at all. One of Aristotle's successors noted in passing that the past is all we have. He was only half right. We have the present that the past made possible. This memoir is one man's view of that possibility."

My suspicion (perhaps I should say my threat) that I might return to the book and extend it has since become a self-fulfilling prophecy. There was a second enlarged edition in 1992, and a third that was enlarged further in 1998. But each of these came into being in the same spirit of serendipity that prompted my writing the book in the first place. On Valentine's Day in 1985 I celebrated the romanticism of the occasion by slipping on a ridge of ice and fracturing my left ankle in three places—a "skier's break" in the glamorous language of the orthopods. After the ankle was set and cast, I was more or less sedentary for some weeks and from that position I could not help but notice how Pittsburgh, having been designated then as the most "livable city in the United States" by Rand McNally, was suddenly being discovered by hired pens and journeying promoters who seemed totally unaware (or at least existentially unaware) of Pittsburgh's past.

Piqued into action because I had lived that through that past and resented its having been slighted, I began to make a few notes about aspects of the city as I remembered them. These notes eventually were transformed into an essay that was published in *Carnegie Magazine*. Embellishing the essay were a number of drawings by Robert Qualters, an artist resident in Pittsburgh then and still.

Eventually I did expand the essay into a book (1986), picked the paper, designed the book in part, printed it at my own expense and was the beneficiary of more of Bob Qualters' distinctive drawings. My original intention was to publish a few hundred copies and use them as gifts to friends and others, but pre-publication orders made me raise the number significantly. The first edition sold out. Four years later the second enlarged edition sold out. And in 1998 the third edition sold out. In addition, I received letters and telephone calls of appreciation that I will treasure as long as I live. Particularly memorable was a telephone call from a man who did not give his name but said succinctly, "I just finished reading your book, and what you did was write the story of my life."

Now that seventeen years have passed between the publication of the first edition and this fourth edition, I must say that what I wrote in the first three editions still seems current to me. For that reason I have not dickered with the text, and the first three editions are presented here exactly as they were when originally published. True, many of the people named in the text have moved on or died, but the character of the city has become even more definite despite some superficial changes. I would ask you to consider the 1986, 1992 and 1998 sections as you would consider untouched photographs that were taken of Pittsburgh at those times. There are, however, two errors in fact in the original text that demand correction. The first has to do with the diameter of the pillars at the Mellon Institute (now integrated into Carnegie Mellon University). I estimated then that the pillars at their base were as large as an opened parachute. In fact, they measure approximately seven feet in diameter. To compare that footage with the diameter of an opened parachute (even a small one) is hyperbole.

The second error is when I misidentify the "crazy birds" over the Liberty Bridge as "wrens or sparrows." After publication I learned from an ornithologist that they are actually European starlings.

In all probability this will be the final edition of *The Pittsburgh That Stays Within You*. Updating is an endless assignment, and at this point it seems wiser to let what I've written stand as written and leave future changes and visions to someone else's pen. After all, this memoir is no more than an interior history of a Pittsburgh as it was and is in my recollection. I simply wrote down, as the book's title suggests, what stayed within me. If this provoked in readers a number of similar or different memories of what stayed and stays within them, then it served its purpose.

Samuel Hazo

Woolworth's, 1975.

1986

Does this memoir begin with daily ladlings of drinking water from the stationary tubs and wringer-topped washing machine in the basement because the St. Patrick's Day flood in the mid-thirties forced the water company to shut down the pipes, creating ten days of no baths? Or does it begin when you walked to high school in the smog? You were barely able to perceive the ghosts of telephone poles as you hurried by them. The mute cars snailed along like vehicles under water, their probing headlights fusing into a single beam before them like eyesight. If you held your hand straight ahead of you in the dawn murk, you could just perceive the vague and flexing fingertips. You arrived at school with your nares filmed and fuzzed with smogsoot, and the white collar of your shirt was outlined with the same film and fuzz. Even though *that* Pittsburgh is forty years dead, it is still the one you hear about from people who prefer to believe that Pittsburgh is what it was and not what it has remarkably become.

Or does this memoir start with the old farmer's market on the downtown bank of the Monongahela where the lemons and oranges and apples were stacked man-high as though each lemon and orange and apple were its own kind of brick in a fruit pyramid, and where, in season, you could buy a live spring lamb, and where your father once did just that and then slaughtered it in the basement over your mother's protests?

All memoirs are fragmentary, and memories of a changing city are more fragmentary than most. The new keeps erasing or transfiguring the old until you think that the past is just something you dreamed. Each remembered fragment becomes a puzzle-piece of a long since disassembled puzzle of a city, but each fragment in time's mysterious metamorphosis has already started to evolve into other fragments, and the changes never end because a city—*any* city—is not so much a place as it is an idea or rather a gathering of ideas where each idea influences every other idea as it inevitably and ineluctably realizes itself, and the resulting ferment and fusion define what we call a city in the similar difference of every ongoing minute . . .

You are playing soccer (called "kickball" then) in the red dog playground in front of Wightman School (now a social center but once one of the finest elementary schools in Pittsburgh under the principalship of a certain Miss Frew), and one of the kickball players seems more accomplished than all the others, and the goalie tells you during a time out that the player is Paul Waner's son, and you say, "Who?" The following year you are sitting well up in the right field stands of Forbes Field (gone now

Forbes Field, 1986.

except for a fragment of the left field wall over which Bill Mazeroski hit the ninth-inning home run that defeated the awesome and unforgiving Yankees in 1960 in what James Reston headlined as "O Cruel and Fateful Acts of Piracy"), and you watch the Pirates win the game with a line double off the right field wall from the bat of Paul Waner (or "Big Poison" to distinguish him, in the argot of the press, from his younger brother Lloyd or "Little Poison"). Exiting from Forbes Field, you think of Waner's son and wonder why you haven't seen him all summer, and the boy with you just says, "Camp," and that will be the last time you will ever mention Waner's son's name because you and everyone else that night have just seen Paul Waner in his last season as a Pirate.

After that there will be so many memories of Forbes Field that you will lose track: the great Koufax pitching or rather throwing when he was still young and wild; Red Schoendienst sizing up the infield as he waits to stand in the batter's box, readying his bat like a pool player chalking his cue; Jackie Robinson spearing a line drive five feet over his head or running the bases as if they belonged to him; the catch that Willie Mays made (Branch Rickey called it Mays' greatest catch and possibly the greatest catch in baseball history) of a Clemente drive into right center field when he ran out of room and at the last second reached out and caught the ball with his bare hand; the uncoiling swing of Stan Musial; the home run that Mickey Mantle, batting right-handed, hit over the right centerfield wall in 1960, a feat previously accomplished by only a handful of left-handed batters; the youthful infield in the Billy Meyer days when it was rumored (in the gospel according to Joe Garagiola) that no one was yet old enough to shave; the colorful and stubborn Pirate team of 1960 and the equally resilient championship team of 1979 which climbed doggedly from last place to first and then defeated the outspoken Orioles in Baltimore.

It is September, years later, and you are walking down South Aiken Avenue where the mayor's house flanks Harriet Street. Mayor David L. Lawrence ("King Davey" to foe and friend alike) is standing on the sidewalk in a gray suit and a gray fedora with the brim up as was the plucky custom among Democrats in the heady days of Roosevelt and Truman, both of whom wore their hats with the brims up. You say, "Good morning," and the mayor smiles and says, "Good morning, young man," and you remember how the mayor's sons were killed in an automobile accident just twelve months earlier. As an adult many years later you will emerge from the Shadyside Theater to learn that former Governor David L. Lawrence suffered a heart attack while speaking at a Democratic rally (an authentic last hurrah), and you will read in the newspapers on the days following the attack how life support systems sustained him until Bishop John Wright (later Cardinal John Wright and certainly one of the most cosmopolitan of all Pittsburgh bishops as well as, curiously, one of the most conservative) advised, when asked, that life should be supported by "ordinary rather than extraordinary means" in such cases, and a day later David Leo Lawrence, a force in Pittsburgh politics as well as state and national affairs for most of his adult life and the man who, along with Mayor Richard Daley of Chicago, delivered the nomination and, some say, the 1960 presidential election to John Fitzgerald Kennedy, is dead.

You remember the Hill. It began at the fringe of downtown and continued in sprawling, byzantine configurations almost to Soho, containing within its perimeters immigrants from Italy, Ireland, Syria, Lebanon, central Europe, a vast population of blacks, a coterie of Jewish merchants in the dry goods business and an institution known as the Home for the Improvement of the Poor where impoverished blacks and whites lived in the integrated society that poverty created and always creates. The Hill was where immigrants and blacks "began." Their children would move out. Some would become famous. Lena Home and recent Academy Award Winner F. (for Fred) Murray Abraham were from the Hill as was Billy Eckstine.

Faleder Monuments, 1980.

But in its prime the Hill was an atmosphere unto itself. On side streets were Italian food shops where necklaces of garlic hung from coat hooks in the ceiling beside gauze-wrapped loaves of hard salami from "the old country," and beneath the dangling spices and meats were barrels of dried fish and bins of immeasurable pasta. Wedged between the food shops were repair nooks where shoemakers pried off old heels and soles and replaced them with new ones (you have a fixed memory of these skilled men with a reserve supply of nails clutched between their lips) or small cubicles where tailors stitched trousers or pressed suitcoats on hissing handpresses. Above their cash registers were posted technicolor photographs of President Franklin Delano Roosevelt seated in front of an American flag. And there was a famous restaurant called Samreny's (it still exists but in a different location, and its clientele is no longer the knowledgeable underground of reporters, salesmen and sharpies but the new gourmets of the middle class who have middled their way to Middle Eastern cuisine) where you could order broiled lamb cubes on a stick or *sheesh* and where men born in Beirut or Jerusalem or the Akar district of Syria played backgammon for

Diamond Market, 1960.

hours, shouting out the dice numbers in Turkish each time they made a cast. Today the whole area is redeveloped. The Civic Arena with its retractable roof is there as are Chatham Center, the Pittsburgh Hyatt, a Medical Pavilion and an expensive high rise called Washington Plaza. The squalor is gone, and that is obviously to the good, but, curiously enough, so is much of the color.

You remember the years of the three dailies—the *Post-Gazette*, the *Press* and the *Hearst Sun-Telegraph* with its lurid American Weekly section every Sunday. And there was also a defiant and literate magazine called the *Bulletin Index*, which was edited briefly in the thirties by novelist John O'Hara and ended with quiet dignity in 1948, but its stylized essays and reports deserve some dispassionate research by someone some day. The *"Tele"* is long dead. The *Post-Gazette* tried briefly to gobble up its Sunday market with its own Sunday edition, but the experiment failed. Now the *Press* and *Post-Gazette* have combined publishing and distribution facilities while managing to keep their editorial policies as disparate as separate languages or theologies. The *Press* emphasizes (along with its new *Washington Post*-like format) that it is familial in its concern for its readership while the *Post-Gazette* describes itself as international in its outlook with a strong local base.

You remember, too, the Church of the Epiphany, which still stands where it once served so many immigrant families as well as tired compositors and late-daters at its 2:00 A.M. Printers' Mass. Its sister church, St. Peter's, has long since been turned into a street. It was rumored that the Epiphany's rector, Father O'Connell, who, in addition to fostering a love for the fiction of Charles Dickens in his parishioners, allegedly had a lot to say in the making of more than one Pittsburgh mayor and whose influence at City Hall, so the story goes, was not negligible, made sure that it was St. Peter's and not the Epiphany that was demolished in the name of urban renewal. You remember when a visiting poet came to Pittsburgh and was hosted in a penthouse office by a cultural leader who had done much of the legal work that made such demolition possible. Seeing the demolition of St. Peter's in progress, the poet turned to the leader and said, "What son of a bitch arranged for that church to be torn down?" Smiling and holding *his* ground, the leader said, "I did." The poet, holding his ground, did not take back a word.

Just below the Epiphany on Fifth Avenue some of the longstanding dry goods stores are being gentrified one by one into single-story or two-story buildings for lawyers who have gotten "sick and tired" of the high rents in the Frick Building and the Union Trust Building (probably the most beautiful office building in the city with its gabled corners, its church-like roof offices and its strong resemblance to a section of the Houses of Parliament) and have decided to do something about it. The result is redevelopment in the best sense imaginable, and the future of that part of Fifth Avenue grows brighter, office by office by office.

You cannot forget the steadfastness of Carnegie Institute and how you went there for the first time in your life one Saturday afternoon and stayed and browsed all day inspecting old arrowheads, models of ships of sail, Indian headdresses, dinosaur bones, a display featuring a killed moose with the arrow that killed it still in its side, trays of precious stones in their rough state, fig-leafed statues of Mercury and some of his brother gods, and, furtively, in a photographic exhibition beside the Hall of Architecture, a standing male and female nude photographed from the rear on a hilltop in what you then considered the "dirtiest" picture you ever saw. Later you would join the Carnegie Library. Your first book as a borrower would be a novel about dogfights during the First World War entitled *Falcons of France*, but you subsequently read all the stories of Dr. Doolittle and Kipling's *Jungle Book*. Many Septembers later, as a high school student, you applied for a job as an usher in Carnegie Music Hall. The ushers in those days wore uniforms that reminded you of the bellhop who became identified as Johnny in the Philip Morris cigarette commercials. You remember, as you walked through the marble foyer of the Music Hall that imposed (and still imposes) its own hush, that you wanted to wear that uniform more than anything. Somebody else got the job.

Of course you could begin this memoir of the change in Pittsburgh with the time you tried to find a motorman in the Pennsylvania Station in order to buy a ticket to Washington, D.C. Once crowded, the station had already started to go the way of many other train stations across the United States. In those days of thinning crowds you could count the passengers for certain departures on one hand and, on this particular night, on one thumb. Still, the prospect of a serious snow in the forecast made it prudent for you to buy a rail ticket in case your flight of the following morning should be cancelled. When you finally smoked out someone in the station who seemed authorized to sell you a ticket, he took your money like a bad debt and muttered sullenly, "When the birds don't fly, then you come to us." You left him with his morose victory while you recalled the halcyon days of rail when you could travel to New York or Rochester or South Bend from that very station or from the Pittsburgh and Lake Erie Terminal across the river. The stations were *stations* then, filled with students, commuters and other passengers who were heading out from Pittsburgh to all the compass points or returning. You measured distances between cities by hours in that era, not minutes, and you would settle back in your coach seat with a book that you could almost finish during the journey, and the conductors in blue twill and squat silo-caps would punch your ticket and stick the punched ticket in the seatback slot just in front of you, thus making you legitimate, and afterward white-capped vendors would swagger through the slightly swaying car with sandwiches wrapped in waxed paper, candy bars and whatever it was they thought was coffee, and, while you were eating and sipping from the coffee cup that you balanced precipitously on the windowsill between sips, you could watch Ohio or Indiana pass by as farm after farm or field after field until cities like Cleveland or Toledo or South Bend would begin to assemble themselves from

Pennsylvania & Lake Erie Railroad Station, 1972.

the suburbs inward to their downtown cores before the train would start up again, and the fleeing panorama of farms and fields and villages would re-appear in the passing vastness of America, and you would find yourself dozing, the book splayed obediently on your lap.

Now both the Pennsylvania Station and the Pittsburgh and Lake Erie Terminal are but relics of their time and original purpose. The P.&L.E. has been remodeled into a restaurant beside the old tracks opposite an imaginative development known as Station Square where you can buy everything from shoes and sporting goods to smokers' pipes and foreign teas and jams. The Pennsylvania Station, a squarish monolith with one of the most beautiful porticos in the city, has been poised for years between re-consecration and the wrecking ball. According to recent reports and rumors, re-consecration is definitely in the offing.

All of the aforementioned is not nostalgia. It is a way of seeing and feeling where and how Pittsburgh became what it is in the mid-80's. Unlike many other cities in this country, which strive to ape the so-called sophistication of New York or the transient and changing cosmopolitanism of Washington or whatever it is that San Francisco is supposed to radiate, Pittsburgh persists in being existentially itself. It simply but inevitably and determinedly keeps becoming what it is. And what it is was enough to earn it kudos recently. Called the most livable city in the United States by a Rand McNally rating committee (much to the consternation of cities like Philadelphia, Boston, Baltimore and Atlanta), Pittsburgh seemed to wear the mantle lightly, if at all. Of course, civic leaders and others were euphoric, but the indigenous Pittsburgher shrugged, smiled and went on with his life. Shortly after the rating was announced, the *Pittsburgh Post-Gazette* conducted a survey in which Pittsburghers were asked to suggest ways in which "the number one city" could be made more attractive to tourists. Answers ranged from planting azaleas on Mt. Washington's slopes to expanding the new but small subway system. One respondent wrote without apology that nothing at all should be done to make Pittsburgh more attractive to tourists since Pittsburgh was not a city that revealed itself readily to tourists but only to residents. And that for her was that.

Lifelong residents of the city tend to measure the new against what preceded it and make their judgments accordingly. As a rule, Pittsburghers do not embrace the new just because it is new. They are more than casually conservative that way, and their ultimate criterion in evaluating the old against the new or vice-versa is to ask the sensible question, "Is it any good?" Take the case of Forbes Field, for example. Deep in tradition, it was where Pie Traynor and his championship team played, where Babe Ruth hit his 714th and final home run on May 25, 1935, where Ralph Kiner hit prodigious homers that made the Pirates interesting if not competitive in the forties, where no Pirate pitcher had ever thrown a no-hitter. Located at the edge of Schenley Park, Forbes Field was in the very heart of Oakland. On one side of it was the lush background of the park. But its real asset was that it was within blocks of restaurants, stores and trolley lines, and enterprising Oakland residents could make a quick dollar or two on game nights by allowing fans to park their cars in driveways and, occasionally, front yards. Because of its location, you could go, as a leading Pittsburgh architect named Tasso Katselas (he was speaking with the stern authority of a fan) observed, to a baseball game on impulse. And many people did just that. They went to a baseball game because they suddenly felt like going to a baseball game. Why? Because it was possible, and what is possible eventually becomes factual.

Torn down to make way for a complex of libraries and other buildings owned by the University of Pittsburgh, Forbes Field continues to haunt the new stadium built to take its place on the North Side. Why the North Side was chosen is a story in itself, but it won out over other sites and plans, including one that envisioned a stadium constructed directly *over* the Allegheny River itself. Multipurposed (ready for everything from sports events to rock concerts to conventions for true believers) and cursed with a generic name (Three Rivers Stadium), the new facility is just that—a new facility. Impulsive attendance is a thing of the past. You must plan to attend. You drive or use various other means to get there; you see the event; you leave. There is no time for kibitzing or lollygagging, and many people prefer not to stay any longer in that area of the North Side than necessary, even if after-the-event sessions of one kind or another are possible. Many Pittsburghers will tell you that Three Rivers Stadium offers function without garnishes and color. Rand McNally rating or no Rand McNally rating, they insist that Forbes Field had the color and the ambience, and nothing anybody can say will change their minds.

Some people in the city still remember when Chancellor Bowman of the University of Pittsburgh encouraged young Pittsburghers to buy a brick for a dime (an *earned* dime) to erect the Cathedral of Learning. The Cathedral of Learning with its lead-lined drainspouts and gutters and its ground-floor galaxy of nationality rooms (Chinese, Czechoslovak, English, French, German, Greek, Hungarian, Irish, Italian, Lithuanian, Norwegian, Polish, Romanian, Russian, Scottish, Syrian-Lebanese, Yugoslav and Early American-with Austrian, Armenian, Ukrainian, African and Israeli heritage rooms on the drawing boards) still dominates the Oakland landscape like an exclamation point. (Nikita Kruschev was impressed by it when he visited the city in 1959 though he could not refrain from saying that Moscow University was bigger—"Mos-cow beeeger").

But the University of Pittsburgh is many other buildings today (it is also the city's largest employer), including the remodeled Hotel Schenley (now the student union and assorted other offices) where Eleanora Duse breathed her last in 1924. One block west are three student dormitories of varying heights but all built like cylinders with the rooms therein some-what pieshaped. The students promptly christened them Ajax, Babo and Comet.

One block east is the Mellon Institute with its façade of limestone pillars that stand more than three-stories high and still intrigue the speculative engineer in you to explain how they were transported by rail from their quarries in the South and erected pillar by pillar to create the Parthenon-like exterior of the building. According to one account, the first pillar was brought to Pittsburgh in two sections (pause and imagine for a moment two sections of cylindrical limestone with each section a story-and-a-half long and the circumference at the base not much smaller than a fully opened parachute). Andrew W. Mellon, one of Pittsburgh's original men of wealth and a Secretary of the Treasury during the Republi-can twenties, ordered the sectioned pillar back to its quarriers and carvers. He wanted each pillar to come in *one* piece (now imagine *that*, and then imagine what it must have taken to erect each one of these monoliths into position). Today this imposing example of Greek *moderne* is a research facility under the administration of Carnegie Mellon University.

The latter, known to this day by its more distant alumni and by ongoing Pittsburghers as "Tech" or "Carnegie Tech," has graduated its fair share of America's distinguished actors and actresses and directors. From an older generation there were Arthur Kennedy, William Eythe and Sada Thomp-son (and too many others to list), and there have been recent graduates like the children of Van Heflin and Harry Belafonte as well as a niece of Katharine Hepburn. A graduate student named John Michael Tebelak conceived the idea for a musical called *Godspell* as partial fulfillment of his master's thesis while he was at Carnegie Mellon more than a decade ago, and many of those associated with a television series called *Hill Street Blues* have Carnegie Mellon connections. Mention the name of Carnegie Mellon or "Carnegie Tech" to the cognoscenti in New York or Los Angeles, and there is immediate recognition of its dramatic tradition. Prominent directors, actors and playwrights often visit for lectures, seminars or residencies. On one occasion a number of years ago the students invited Arthur Miller to make an appearance there. At that time Miller was married to Marilyn Monroe. The students concluded their letter of invitation to Miller by chivalrously including a sentence that he should feel free to bring Mrs. Miller with him.

Today, Carnegie Mellon, under the presidency of Richard M. Cyert, plans to buttress its solid reputation in its major areas with future developments in electronics, computers and software. Years ago football was de-emphasized. The current teams are playing in a much more measurable league, and the era of Merlyn Condit and Virgil Cantini (recruited by Tech as a quarterback and now a practicing artist and sculptor in Pittsburgh whose creations adorn many a Pittsburgh building or plaza and many more a Pittsburgh home) is part of what linguists would call the preterit or definite past. When the decision was made to get Tech out of big-time football, the students marched on the home of then President Doherty on Morewood Avenue with blood in their undergraduate eyes. Doherty emerged from his house and, holding his easel in one hand and a moist paintbrush in the other, confronted the multitudes who already had him swinging in effigy from a hoisted broom handle in their midst and said calmly, "Gentlemen, perhaps you may have come to the wrong school." And with that he turned and went back to the more important matter of the painting he was in the process of completing.

As someone with more than a casual interest in language, you cannot recall when you first became aware of American as it is spoken in Pittsburgh. But no commentary on Pittsburgh would be complete without passing reference to the indigenous dialect. Books and articles have been written about "Pittsburghese" in which it is duly noted that "Irish" is pronounced as a single syllable, and East Liberty is elided into "Sliberty." But the most distinctive characteristic of "Pittsburghese" is that the verb *to be* is often (some would say poetically) understood. Pittsburghers, for example, think nothing of saying "The car needs washed" or "His hair needs cut." Grammarians from elsewhere quickly note that the object of the verb in such constructions is and should be a gerund, *i.e.*, "The car needs washing" or "His hair needs cutting." Local grammarians nod and say with a touch of annoyance that the verb *to be* is understood. Additional proclivities could be listed, such as "Redd-up the table" (translation: make ready or clean off the table), but they are now cliches to Pittsburghers although those not from the city are more mystified than amused by such usage. A recent mayor of Pittsburgh, Peter ("Pete") Flaherty, spoke "Pittsburghese" with such a decided accent that he could be immediately identified in Washington or elsewhere as being from no other city than the one he was from. In conclusion, most linguists agree that the best way to spot a Pittsburgher is to ask him to pronounce "downtown" or "wash." The "o's" in "downtown" are somewhere between the "a" in "father" and the "a" in "tan" but not quite, and the "a" in "wash" is something short of the "oi" in "oink" and the sound of a muted burp. In both cases, the diphthong has yet to be coined or named that is the exact equivalent of such sounds.

It was after you read John Marquand's *The Late George Apley* a second time that you began to theorize about the many ways that Pittsburgh resembles Boston. (Boston, incidentally, is America's second most livable city in the Rand McNally scheme of things). Like Boston, Pittsburgh was once the fiefdom of the Pittsburgh counterparts of the Cabots and the Lodges and the Lowells. The names of Carnegie, Westinghouse, Mellon, Scaife, Frick, Schenley, McCandless and Schwab were the *lingua franca* of power in the city. Economically, this is probably still true in the scions and inheritors of the gentry legacy, and Pittsburgh has benefited from the enlightened philanthropy of many of these men and their families or executors in ways that are beyond comparison, including the major efforts of the Heinz family and their various foundations.

But gradually the Irish immigrants and their children started to make themselves felt in politics, in the church, in the fire and police departments and in other leadership positions (as was the case in post-Apley Boston) so that for decades after their power was consolidated, the names of mayors, bishops, police chiefs and fire chiefs were Irish—Canevin, Boyle, Scully, Lawrence, Kane, Flaherty, Dearden, Wright and so on. The economic "haves" moved either to Fox Chapel or Sewickley or Ligonier, maintaining their economic interests in the city but consigning political and ancillary forms of social power to the well organized and more numerous Irish. Some ethnic shifts have appeared lately, though the years when ward bosses could turn out a predictable vote are less and less common. Regardless, the Democratic density of the city core seems to be constant as is the pattern known as the "Balkan Succession" by which members of city council are chosen according to their racial, ethnic or religious identities. For years it was a common form of political comedy to ask the name of the Republican candidate in the mayoralty election. Few among the electorate knew, and most didn't care since the conclusion was foregone anyway.

Republicans who did run in such hopeless cases justified their being in the race by claiming that they were doing it for the party. Only the annals of political martyrdom remember who they were.

The most significant rapprochement of political and economic power in the city occurred during the mayorship of David L. Lawrence and the economic swayship of Richard K. Mellon. As is now nationally known and extolled, both men allied their constituencies to rid Pittsburgh once and for all of its smog problem and to create a genuine renaissance in the downtown area. The result was a transformation of truly historical proportions. Not only was the air rinsed, but large areas of the Golden Triangle and adjacent sections were changed "utterly" and for the better. A building known as Gateway I was soon followed by its ordinally similar namesakes. Conrad Hilton bided his time and then built his hotel broadside near the Point so that the first thing that visitors would see when they entered the city through the Fort Pitt Tunnel would be the golden Hilton facade, which is precisely what Mr. Hilton intended them to see.

Such an entrance, by the way, must qualify as one of the most dramatic ways of entering any city in the world (aside from the cablecar descent from the top of the Venezuelan Andes into Caracas), and this is even more pointedly the case today with the addition of such new skyscrapers as the PPG Building, the Oxford Centre and the Mellon Bank building. All three were under simultaneous construction as part of Pittsburgh's Renaissance II, and bystanders watched them evolve upward from their respective locations near Market Square, opposite the Grant Building and directly across Fifth Avenue from the Court House until they bloomed together in a re-designed skyline of their own creation. Observing this skyline from the Fort Pitt Bridge or the Liberty Bridge or from the Parkway East as it swerves past the Oakland Exit, you have a definite sense, not of megalopolis as you have when you loop Dallas on the LBJ eight-laner, but of metropolis.

As one of those who make the trip into Pittsburgh daily through the Fort Pitt Tunnel, you know what it's like to enter the usual traffic patterns on the western side of Mt. Washington (originally called Coal Hill because the most valuable deposit of bituminous coal in the entire United States was discovered there in 1760) before you are funneled through the two-laned, tile-sided tubes and reborn a mile or so later with the entire downtown skyline as well as the North and South Sides and the confluence of the Monongahela and Allegheny that sire the Mississippi-destined Ohio all in front of you. You never seem to tire of it. (Coming home in the evening is another story entirely. The traffic is heavy, though not as heavy as that on the Parkway East heading for Monroeville, and you always wonder about the intelligence quotient of the highway engineer who was inspired to fuse six highspeed traffic lanes from three different directions into the turbulent headwaters of the downtown end of the Fort Pitt Bridge).

By daylight the experience of coming into the city through the Fort Pitt Tunnel is mercurial and stunning. By night there is a sense of sophistication and romance that must be lived in order to be understood. Similarly, if you decide to have dinner or just saunter along Grandview Avenue atop Mt. Washington at night, you might be lucky enough to do so on the night when all the office buildings in downtown Pittsburgh have their lights on. The resulting sweep of unrelieved illumination is enough to deepen your gratitude to Thomas Alva Edison forever.

If, after crossing the Fort Pitt Bridge, you veer to the left and skirt the downtown area, you eventually arrive at a section known familiarly as The Strip. One travel writer once referred to certain food-producing areas of France as "the breasts of the country." Using this writer's succulent metaphor, it is possible by transposition to claim that The Strip is the breasts of Pittsburgh. Cheese, produce, fish, meat, pasta, gourmet condiments, olives by the barrel, desserts, plants—they are all in abundance for the buying. But what makes any visit to The Strip an occasion is the atmosphere. It's the Allegheny County counterpart of Les Halles in Paris. This is not the cellophane-wrapped and computerized shopping of the supermarkets. This is vending or, in some cases, hawking. You pick your own tomatoes and cucumbers. You browse. You argue. You ask, innocently enough, if the owner of one of the open-air food markets has long-leafed parsley. His answer is, "Can ducks swim?" You enter. You feel the sawdust under your soles. You pass the sprinkled lettuce, the green peppers that Edward Weston photographed as having the lines of female nudes, the old-fashioned scales that have a gondola chain swung below a clocklike register of pounds, the zebra-striped watermelons, yesterday's peaches on special, lemons and limes brothered in the same bin. The owner wraps your long-leafed parsley in last week's front page and wordlessly takes your money. As you turn away, you hear him tell you, "We always have that stuff. When you want it, it's here. Remember that." You leave, fortifying yourself for the next purchase.

If you go to The Strip early in the morning, at predawn if possible, you can buy cheaper and fresher what will be more costly and less fresh at neighborhood markets later in the day. There is a lot of shouting and bickering, most of it good-natured, some of it spirited, some cantankerous, none really malicious. It's the give and take that enlivens you. When you need a respite, you can stop at Primanti's or Wholey's or Benkowitz's for a sandwich that is second to none and then return to the fray. Eventually you leave with the feeling that you've dealt with food at its distributive source (the metaphor of the breasts can be overworked at this point, but in fact you've been as close to the source as city people can get) and that you've gotten the most for your money, which is as much of a satisfaction to people in a capitalistic society as the profit motive itself. Well, almost as much of a satisfaction . . . .

Departing from The Strip, you go straight out Penn Avenue for several miles, passing Doughboy Square and the Allegheny Cemetery (Pittsburgh's *Pére Lachaise* where Lillian Russell is buried). Eventually you reach East Liberty. At present East Liberty is an example of what bad urban planning (and, some critics add, amateurish governmental interference) can do to a once prosperous commercial center. You remember what it was to be a teenager in East Liberty on a Saturday afternoon. You might go to a matinee at the Sheridan Square or the Regent or the Enright Theater and, if you were eating an ice cream cone, you would be politely asked to finish eating the cone before going to your seat. You remember Joyce-McClements, a restaurant and catering institution that made, according to Peter Bolanis, a longstanding maker of chocolate in the same area today and one of the few remaining quality merchants who survived in East Liberty, the best ice cream in the world. When Bolanis was approached by representatives of

East Liberty Bus Station, 1984.

Häagen-Dazs to carry their line of flavors in his store, he answered without rancor or sarcasm that they did not know what good ice cream really was because they had never tasted the flavors that Joyce-McClements used to make.

A flavor called bisque stands out in your memory—crushed cashews (or was it pecans?) blended into unconscionably rich vanilla ice cream. When you worked there one summer, you used to go to the ice cream coolers downstairs where the newly made ice cream was jelling and scoop a cup of bisque or coffee or butter pecan (it was not yet ice cold and had the consistency of apple butter) and sip or chug-a-lug it like ambrosia. And this is not meant to slight Joyce-McClements' whipped cream cake, which still causes rememberers to salivate when they speak of it. You remember the family-owned department store (Mansmann's), the stationery shop (Harrison Hays), the haberdashery which carried a full line of separate collars (Aufhammer and Evans, Roy V. Beese, Proprietor), the food market (Donahoe's), the jeweler's (Henne's) and countless other places of business whose good name rested on years of excellent merchandising and honest service.

And they were accessible to the public because East Liberty was accessible. Now the traffic patterns that were designed for the new East Liberty seem to have had as their goal the total avoidance of the area itself. It really takes a decisive mental effort to drive your way into and out of the place now. Many of the stores that are not out of business and covered with buckboard and graffiti are as far removed from the old sense of quality as the so-called new East Liberty is from the East Liberty that it regrettably replaced. (If you detect in this paragraph this Pittsburgher's inclination to eschew the new in favor of the older and better, you are correct, and the fact that I am an erstwhile East Libertarian has more than a little to do with it). On the Rand McNally scale of livability, East Liberty seems today to be one area that hurt Pittsburgh more than it helped it, but the fault lay with the "overviewers" and not with the true East Libertarians. In fact, it would not be surprising to find the next East Liberty as a regeneration of the old in accordance with the maxim that all it takes to scrub a bad idea is a good idea. Now that the redoubtable Motor Square Garden (used formerly as a Foodshow center and an auto palace) is being re-designed as a major shopping mall, it seems that the regeneration has already begun.

Everyone regrets the elimination of a landmark, regardless of the reasons. The old Nixon Theater on Sixth Avenue was *the* theater in Pittsburgh at one time for quite a long time. Traveling companies would present Broadway plays there on a regular basis. Audiences in the Nixon's three-tiered seating sections saw and heard most of the great stage actresses and actors of the first half of the twentieth century—Lunt and Fontanne, Katherine Cornell, Maurice Evans and Burgess Meredith, to name only a few. You yourself recall seeing the first road company perform a surprise musical success called *Oklahoma* there. You saw Boris Karloff in *Arsenic and Old Lace* and later interviewed him backstage in his dressing room where his reserve and his gentlemanliness made a deep impression on you. You remember the towering presence of Louis Calhern in a now forgotten play called *Jacobowsky and the Colonel* (Calhern was the colonel) as well as a fine production of *A Streetcar Named Desire* with Anthony Quinn and Uta Hagen.

Two drama critics ruled Pittsburgh in those days. One was Harold V. (it stood for nothing as in Harry S. Truman) Cohen of the *Pittsburgh Post-Gazette*. The other was Kaspar Monahan of the *Pittsburgh Press*. Both men were recipients of major awards for their criticism of film and theater, and the Pittsburgh reading public for years was the beneficiary of their pithy work. Today that literate tradition is carried on with equal distinction by George Anderson of the *Pittsburgh Post-Gazette* and Ed Blank of the *Pittsburgh Press*.

After the demise of the Nixon and a short-lived attempt to continue the tradition in a re-located Nixon, theater lovers had not much reason to attend plays locally. Various attempts were made to start and maintain a repertory theater under Bill Ball and various others, but it was not until the establishment of the Pittsburgh Public Theater that viability became a fact for a significant theatrical presence in Pittsburgh. The new Benedum Theater, it is hoped, will do for Pittsburgh in the last decades of this century and beyond what the old Nixon did for Pittsburgh in the earlier decades. The new theater will not have the old Hotel Henry (now the site of Mellon Square and a labyrinthine underground parking garage) in its orbit for pre-performance and postperformance dining, but there will surely be other compensations if visionaries like H. J. Heinz, Robert Dickey, Carol Brown and their associates have anything to say about it. And they will.

You also remember how the Pittsburgh Symphony was housed for years in the Syria Mosque before it moved into the house that Heinz built by literally re-creating the Loew's Penn Theater and dubbing it Heinz Hall. You learned only recently that the symphony was originally intended to be headquartered in the Carnegie Music Hall in Carnegie Institute.

This superbly foyered hall was abandoned by the Symphony after it was learned that the hall was simply too small for it (costs could not be amortized from ticket income even if all the concerts were sold out). Carnegie Music Hall still remains a gem of a hall, and plans are now afoot to attract more users. The Syria Mosque now accomodates a variety of renters, but few are of the stature of those of yester-decades. You cannot forget a performance there of Benet's *John Brown's Body* with Anne Baxter, Judith Anderson, Raymond Massey and Tyrone Power. Power, in a performance that transcended anything he ever did on the screen, stole the show. But such dramatic highlights were only occasional. The Pittsburgh Symphony Orchestra in those years was the Mosque's main tenant. Fritz Reiner was a perennial before the baton was passed on to William Steinberg. You once saw Igor Stravinsky conduct his *Petrouchka* there, his metronomic manner of directing the orchestra with one finger in marked contrast with Steinberg's jowl-shaking thrusts and bows and left hooks.

You are reminded of Duquesne Gardens (why was it plural when Madison Square Garden in Manhattan and the old Motor Square Garden in East Liberty were singular?) and how for years it served as home ice for hockey teams, as a rink of skaters, as a basketball court for college teams, as a tennis court for touring professionals, as a field house for entertainers. Bob Hope played the Gardens once and never quite recovered from it. It—the Gardens—was a block long and had all the interior atmosphere of a car barn. There was a main floor, and there was an overhanging mezzanine of seats that jutted over the main floor, and that was all. You remember sitting in that mezzanine to watch the late Sihugo Green pace an underdog Duquesne University team to a victory over Dayton University. You remember seeing Jack Kramer defeat Bobby Riggs (the same Bobby Riggs who years later conned the American public into taking seriously his bizarre match with Billie Jean King) in one of the ongoing duels that they carried on nationwide for months at a time. Kramer, the more powerful and taller of the two, was extended to the extreme because the countervolleying Riggs assumed all the assets of a wall that returned everything that Kramer hit to him simply by being there.

Playing in a preliminary on that card was a young Latin American named Pancho Segura. His hair was Indian black, and he had the profile of a conquistador. In his white tennis shirt and shorts he looked so much more definite than the other Caucasians that he gradually became the only one worth watching. And he made everyone look twice at the way he two-handed his racquet like a bat and zipped forehand and backhand drives over the net with a velocity and accuracy that traditional hitters thought impossible. Most critics and observers in that era thought that the two-handed practice would probably be confined to Segura. But decades later no one showed the least surprise when Jimmy Connors hit two-handed forehand and backhand shots with even greater accuracy and velocity. His coach? Pancho Segura.

The era of Duquesne Gardens was also the era of the old, orange trolley cars. Seemingly made of cast iron and faced angularly with wooden, orange panels, these cars moved on steel wheels over steel rails with the omnipresence of battleships. Their sides were straight up, and their fronts and rears were tri-faced. The floors of the interior were ridged wood, and the passengers sat on rattan, pew-like seats in the front half of the car so that they faced one another across the intervening aisle. From mid-door to the rear of the car, passengers sat facing forward in dual seats separated by a narrow passage that led to the semi-circle of seats in the very rear. The top of each aisle-seat in this rear area was edged with a small bronze grip for those left standing or for those others who had to wend their way to the front or back while the trolley was in motion. Walking down the wobbling aisle was not unlike negotiating the deck of a pitching ship. Many were the wenders who careened into someone's lap or were sent reeling fro and to as the trolley lurched or made a swing turn.

The trolley conductor sat enthroned, also on rattan, and separating him from the passengers on crowded days was what looked like a gray, rubber, shower curtain. Under the conductor's right hand was a wooden-knobbed gearshift that moved in a fixed circle like an enlarged version of a model train transformer. This was where the electric current was controlled, and circling the shift clockwise or counterclockwise accelerated or decelerated the trolley. With his left hand the conductor would periodically yank down on what resembled an old commode chain that dangled from the ceiling. That was the klaxon. With each yank it clanged, and the conductor always gave it more than one yank. There was a time when the trolleys were manned by two motormen—one to drive the trolley and another to take fares at mid-door. The mid-door motorman made change by clicking out dimes or nickels from a changer at his belt while the driver watched the boarding passengers at the front deposit their tokens or coins in a steel-mouthed till. Eventually the mid-door motorman was dropped, and the mid-door was used only for debouching, allowing an occasional student without a nickel to his name to sneak onto the car in the hope that the driver would not see him in the tactically angled mirror above his seat.

Invariably there were those times when the trolley bar on the roof would somehow slip off the electrified wire that channeled the power into the car itself. At such times the conductor would debark and proceed to the rear of the stalled car and, by jimmying the guideline that controlled the bar itself, would carefully thread the pulley back into contact with the wire and, *voilà*, the car would hum into life again, the lights would come on, and the passengers would give the conductor a round of applause when he re-boarded.

As the trolleys were slowly phased out and as their orange presences disappeared one by one from the Belgian block streets of the city (and now the blocks have largely disappeared or been asphalted from view), they were gradually replaced by red-and-white more streamlined models and currently by accordioning and non-accordioning buses. The latter are certainly more comfortable, commodious and less noisy, but you somehow hoped that their orange predecessors were destined for something more than the scrap heap. A few are enshrined in a trolley museum in Washington, Pennsylvania (Little Washington, as it is known to Western Pennsylvanians) but the rest of them will, like the original highbreasted Coca-Cola glasses or like the Pierce Arrow or the Packard and Hudson and Nash, live forever in the noiseless museums of memory. To all who rode them, the orange trolleys stood not only for themselves but for a solidity and dependability that kept life firmly and permanently on the earth where it seemed to belong.

The Jenkins Arcade, demolished now together with an adjacent building to make room for the new Hillman building, is a memory unto itself. It formed a natural transit between Penn and Liberty Avenues, between Joseph Home's and the vortex of Fifth and Liberty. Passing through the Jenkins Arcade was something like walking through a train station or a European mall. You felt that you were moving, actually moving through time. Of course, you were aware of the aisle of shops, and occasionally, en route to an appointment with a dentist or a doctor on the upper floors, you stopped in some of them for shoes, glasses, leathergoods, fresh bread, haberdashery and an opulence of candy from everywhere that candy came from in one particular store that was never without customers.

The only arcade of sorts that exists from an older era is the one or ones on the groundfloor of the Union Trust Building. The intersecting passages are shortcuts from Kaufmann's to the Westin William Penn or from Grant Street to the Mellon Bank building. But you do not loiter in the arcades of the Union Trust Building even though there are some places of business there. You pass over its white marble floors and exit. Once outside you try to appreciate the baroque-Gothic style of the structure. No building in Pittsburgh impresses you more than this one for the intricacies of its stonework, the dignity (there is no other word) of its windows, the stateliness of its façades. Inside, its rotunda enforces the image of stateliness. If you had an appointment in, say, the offices of Reed, Smith, Shaw & McClay (now re-located in the refurbished Duquesne Light Building), you proceeded through an abundance of mahogany and marble so polished and of such obvious quality that you had a fleeting sense that you were in a counterpart of the Vatican.

Who was it who told you that the International Exhibition of Art began as a result of a conflict of egos? It so happened, the storyteller said, that Andrew W. Mellon and Henry Clay Frick went to Europe to shop for paintings. The trip was at Frick's instigation. Mellon felt that Frick knew more about art than he did, and the result was that he was uncomfortable because of his artistic ignorance as the two of them went from gallery to gallery and salon to salon. Mellon eschewed any number of paintings by the Impressionists simply because he did not care for them although he could have owned almost any of them for a pittance at that time. The one painting that he did like well enough to buy was Georges Rouault's *The Old*

Jenkins Arcade, 1988.

King. This painting is still in the permanent collection and is constantly on
loan even though Rouault's dark oils are beginning to crack so that up
close the painting looks as if it were composed of thousands of puzzle
pieces. Nonetheless, Mellon returned to the United States determined
that he would foster a collection that would rival and eclipse Frick's. He
suggested to an aide that an international art show should be initiated on
an annual basis and that the winners and a few honorable mentions be
purchased as the start of a permanent collection in the Carnegie Institute.
Fiat! The International was begun, and it continues to this day.

Changing a city's architecture is one of the basic ways of changing the
"feel" of a city, and in Pittsburgh, as in every other city, the process is
ongoing. Unlike parts of London and Paris, for example, where interiors of existing structures may be gutted and recreated while the façades
of these structures must remain by law untouched, Pittsburgh seems to
follow a less rigid policy of urban and structural planning. The result is
that the re-construction of many areas results in an almost completely
new geography by creating a different sense of the same space, sometimes
for the better as with certain developments on the Mexican War streets on
the North Side, sometimes for the worse as with the ill-conceived mall in
East Liberty.

Duquesne University, for example, is a good example of how total
renewal changed the very ambience of the campus. Originally this campus
on the bluff overlooking the old Try Street Terminal and the upper section
of downtown was a conglomeration of houses and made-over old structures where the various departmental faculties were quartered. Private
house ownership still existed, and the mixture of students, faculty and
resident civilians was a fact of daily life for decades. Once the homeowners
were bought out by the right of eminent or some other form of domain,
the houses were demolished, and university buildings in the form of a
student union, a music school, a dormitory or two and a science building took their places. The problems were many, as Henry J. McAnulty, the
Holy Ghost priest who was the president during that era and is now the
chancellor, will attest. But the result was a new university, architecturally
speaking, for the presidency of Father Donald S. Nesti. This newly created
space imposed different habits on those living and working in that space,
and these habits were in many ways totally different from the habits of
those who lived and worked there before the change took place. Former
students and teachers walked to classes via alleyways and side streets
while the new generation ambled down a university walk that striped the

campus like Main Street.

It is November 22, 1963, and you are working in your office at Duquesne University when your secretary enters a bit too quietly and says, "Have you heard the President's been shot?" You look up skeptically. It is the start of a new age in your own and in the country's history, but you do not know it yet. You keep on working, but it is purely perfunctory. Your mind is spinning like tires in soft snow. You gradually notice that a definite quiet has established itself in the hallway. You can glimpse students starting to gather in small groups, huddling but saying little. Radios are being turned on in one office after another. You still keep working at your desk, assuring yourself that the shot only wounded the President. The full dimension of the event is not yet apparent to you. When you finally look up, you see a colleague standing in the doorway. "He's dead," he says, and there is absolute certainty in his tone. "Chet Huntley just announced it on NBC." You absorb the news with the same disbelief you experienced when, as a boy of ten in a hockey practice, you fell and heard a bone in your right forearm snap. You just looked at the bent part of your arm, felt it, held it and, knowing the truth, refused it, but the arm stayed broken.

Your colleague says nothing. An ex-Army officer, he looks drawn but certain of what he has told you. He has the look of a man who has heard bad news before in his life. Then he leaves, and you look out of habit at your appointment book and see that you have a meeting in Oakland. More out of instinct or custom than anything else, you leave the office, and in minutes you are driving up Fifth Avenue. Traffic is moving at its usual pace. You wonder how many of the drivers have their car radios on, how many of them know what has happened, how many of them, like yourself, are proceeding with their plotted day for lack of an alternative, a willingness to come to terms with the news, whatever. The car radio beside the never-used cigarette lighter in front of you is all Dallas, the assassination, Mrs. Kennedy, the doctors at the hospital, Pierre Salinger, the Dallas Chief of Police, senators and government officials in Washington. Your appointment, or rather your desire to keep your appointment, evaporates en route. Now you notice that traffic seems to be moving more slowly, almost in slow motion. By the time you return to the campus, many of the students have voluntarily and spontaneously gathered in the chapel. They are kneeling in complete silence. You find a telephone and call your wife. She tells you tearfully that she's heard.

Within half an hour you realize that the work you planned to do is impossible, and you drive home. History is beginning to catch up to you.

You only have an inkling of how profoundly history and the whole democratic process will be affected by one man with a cheap rifle. You try to imagine what tomorrow will be like without Kennedy in office, and the day after that, and the day after that. You realize how much you admired him. You voted for him with a will in an election whose final closeness mystified you. Nixon's shallowness and jingo-ism seemed so palpable. You do not realize it yet, but your vote in 1960 will be the last presidential vote you will make with anything approaching full conviction.

You notice now that the roads are filled with automobiles. It's as if everyone has decided to go home at the same time. You stop at a red-light on Banksville Road, and a newsboy approaches you with a copy of the *Pittsburgh Press* in hand. The headline looks like an enlarged funeral announcement: KENNEDY ASSASSINATED. Below the headline is a photograph of the President, an official photograph, face front. You buy the paper. (You still have it). Ahead of you will be hours of television—black-and-white television, which will match the mood of the weekend. You will watch queues of mourners serpentining around the closed coffin in the coffin-centered rotunda, a group of high school girls in tears, a black Marine corporal saluting the coffin as only a black Marine corporal can salute, the Sunday murder of Oswald, the requiem at St. Matthew's, the sight of Charles de Gaulle at Gallic attention in uniform, the drummed march to Arlington. Years later you will visit St. Matthew's and see the plaque in the floor before the altar where the "remains" of John F. Kennedy rested before the burial. And on a visit to Dallas you will be driven past the Texas Schoolbook Depository and down the boulevard to the underpass. On television the distance from the top of the boulevard to the underpass seemed quite long; in actual fact the distance is so short that you are amazed. Oswald had to have been an excellent shot or lucky.

Your Pittsburgh memories of Kennedy were created during the fight for the nomination and the equally difficult contest of the campaign. During the nomination Kennedy was leaving the William Penn Hotel when a woman, holding a martini in her hand in the hall, deliberately toppled the drink on him, glass and all. Kennedy wiped the martini from his lapel, reached down, picked up the unbroken glass and handed it back to the woman, saying with a smile that was not a smile, "You dropped your glass." During the campaign Kennedy had his motorcade stop in one of the suburbs so that he could visit with a nun and her students who had gathered at the curb to watch the candidate when he passed. Today a statue of Kennedy exists on that very spot.

On the evening of November 22, 1963, as the news sank in, television crews from the various stations were stopping people in downtown Pittsburgh for their reaction to the killing, a form of grisly inquiry that somehow has become a regrettable part of any American tragedy. One woman, obviously of foreign birth to judge by her accent, was in tears as she walked by the interviewer. The interviewer and his cameraman followed her, undissuaded, and pressed her for her thoughts. Without stopping and still in tears she said, "Terrible, terrible. So young man with young wife, and so young children. We are animals, animals." And she walked on without turning her face to the voyeuring camera, without caring.

Turning from tragedy to the city itself, you become personal for a moment. When a city is your home or when you are at home in a city, you take umbrage at innuendoes. You defend it instinctively against denigration. You even exaggerate its good points while you mitigate its bad. But quaffing the heady wine of civic pride cannot and should not blind you to the fact that cities—*all* cities—are in various stages of crisis today. The very history of cities makes you more and more aware of their vulnerabilities day by day. True, the city (assuming, of course, that man is a social animal and that his destiny is to live interdependently with others) can be viewed as man's ultimate civic achievement. Even Plato was firm on that point although he believed with equal firmness that a viable city should not contain more than 5,000 souls—the population of a small town by today's standards.

What is becoming daily more apparent is that the basis for the original creation of most American cities is shifting. Pittsburgh, for instance, became what it is because of its position vis-a-vis the juncturing rivers here and the large deposits of bituminous coal in the area, which made possible the smelting down of iron ore from Minnesota and elsewhere in the coke-fueled open hearths of the steel companies based here for that very purpose. The ethnic diversity of Pittsburgh's population has its roots in those immigrants who created the work force that made such manufacturing possible in the last part of the nineteenth and the first half of the twentieth century.

Today the change in Pittsburgh's economic orientation makes its original geographical assets no longer of primary interest. The result is that perceptive urban planners who are aware of this change are asking questions about its future that parallel the questions being asked by their counterparts in other cities whose identities were forged by the Industrial Revolution. Are cities to be regarded only as places where people work?

What is the purpose of streets? Can the automobile ever be ignored in intelligent urban planning? Will highrise apartments be the vertical neighborhoods or the tenements of the future? What does a city owe to its poor? Are cultural expressions of civic life a mere ornament or refinement, or are they at the very core of what it means to live in a city? These are but a few of the questions, and the answers to these questions will not come from instant specialists or experts but from urban philosophers who understand that a city can create or re-create itself only if it remains aware of its history and the good of its population. It may be that certain cities will not survive but will slowly become counterparts of the old western ghost-towns, abandoned to the changing winds that slowly eroded them as they rose and abated, banging the swinging doors of their deserted taverns like a perpetual last applause. Or will it be that some cities will become ungovernable because of amorphous growth and the erosion of public trust?

In this regard no less a writer than Robert Penn Warren, as perceptive a social critic and historian as he is a poet and writer of fiction, has noted that the Jeffersonian dream is capable of turning into the Jacksonian night-

A Wintry Welcome, 1988.

mare since democracy is not a "mystique" but simply an "arrangement" and quite possibly even a "gamble." Or will it be that American cities, like Pittsburgh, will experience in their renaissance the recurrent myth of the phoenix that regenerated itself continually from its own ashes? After all, was it not Troy itself that had seven or more lives, with each new Troy hatching from the very dust of its predecessors?

Enough speculation. Back to the existential. Specifically, back to the existentialism of snow. City snow. The fact is that city snow differs from country snow, mountain snow, snow on the surface of the sea, snow on snow. City snow ages quickly. And it even more quickly becomes sordid. After the first virginal limning, it hardens into a gray ice if the thermometer stays low enough, or it runs into slush or other forms of city slop. It deprives us of the experience of all color except its own, and its own plays a quick diminuendo from eggshell white to mouse gray. A city like Pittsburgh responds to the snow by falling into the mentality of defense. It begins by budgeting thousands of dollars annually for snow removal. This means crews, equipment, salt, storage areas, vehicle maintenance and the like. During heavy snows a war-like atmosphere is created. The crews move into position with their ploughs and salt spreaders. The snow is the enemy. It must be defeated, and defeat means that it must be furrowed

Goodbye, 1986.

to the sides of roads and highways, shoveled into shunts, melted before
it turns into ice, removed, removed, removed. Why? The answer is quite
frankly that snow does not belong in a city. It is by definition a problem,
and like a problem it must be solved, and usually it must be solved quickly.
It fouls up parkways, airports, places of business, sidewalks, football fields,
drainage systems, automobiles, bridges, parks and whatever it left to its
weighty mercies. Yet it is undeniable. It must be dealt with.

Of course, in the problemless world of the young, snow is the element
of fun. You sled on it. You go galoshing through it. You declare and wage
snowball wars with it. You roll it into bass-drum sized masses, then place
one packed mass atop another, and you perch a basketball of snow on top
of that, and you have the start of a snowman. The piece of broken twig in
his mouth is his cigar, and the two pebbles above his sculpted nose are eyes
that seem to see everything.

According to the most snow-inured Pittsburgher, the principal legacies
of a hard winter are potholes. In Pittsburgh these legacies are frequently
much larger than pots. They have been known to cause everything from
blow-outs to false alignments to accidents. At the very least they are a
boon to mechanics who deal in front wheel alignment. At the worst they
are a cause for accusation after accusation. Some Pittsburghers blame city
planners and elected officials for paving city streets with inferior asphalt.
Others charge that the cause is improper drainage. Still others claim with
some wisdom that the problem is endemic, namely, that sudden freezes
and quick thaws followed by sudden freezes and quick thaws cause the
various surfacings to swell and crack, and then the traffic does the rest. In
mid-March when the central ravages of winter are beginning to slip into
memory and the potholes are at their unrepaired worst, the imaginative
range of driver blasphemy has been known to reach almost Shakespear-
ian heights. The chief result, however, is bluster. By April the potholes are
patched willy-nilly in preparation for serious re-surfacing, and Pittsburgh
drivers, whose memories are short, are heading for Spring and pastures
new.

Despite all the negatives that have been mounted against city snow, there
is one moment (and usually one moment only) when it approaches poetry.
This is the moment after the snow has fallen evenly all night, and you wake
at 6:00 A.M. to a world somehow enhanced and doubled by whiteness. At
that moment there are two telephone wires—one black on the bottom,
one white on top of it. The branches of all the trees are outlined in white.
Ditto: chimneys, garbage can lids, rainspouts, iron or cedar backyard fur-

niture that has been left to the weather. At 6:00 A.M. only the salt crews
have been out, and they have violated the snow's virginity only on the
roads and streets. Everywhere else the snow lies as fallen without a human
footprint to interrupt it. Of course, there are always the careful footprints
of dogs or raccoons or an itinerant deer which has somehow meandered
into the woodsy suburbs. And invariably there is the orange-yellow funnel
in the snow where a dog has urinated and which continues to steam like
a spillage of hot beer. But otherwise the morning snow-world is pristine,
and you walk or drive into it with a sense of wonder and satisfaction that
only such a moment can create, but you know that the moment is passing
even as you savor it.

Snow-stories. You remember a winter in the late seventies when not a
flake of snow had fallen by the first week of January. The winds had been
moderately cold, but the various storms that had been spawned in Canada
had somehow bypassed Pittsburgh. Pittsburghers reacted to this deliver-
ance in two ways. There was one small group of *carpe diem* practitioners
who shrugged at the snowlessness, smiled and enjoyed the respite with
no thought of what the future might or might not bring. Then there was
another and larger group (call them the neo-Calvinists or the eternal wor-
riers whose sense of doom, as the Greeks say, is always strongest when
things are going very well) who faced the snowlessness, frowned and said
more in menace than in prophecy, "No snow yet, but it's coming." In
fact, that particular winter was almost completely devoid of snow from
December through March. But the two attitudes toward the lack of snow
somehow typify two disparate ways of looking at life. The first attitude
is by far the more admirable and even the more realistic. Life is accepted
for what it is right now, not as what it might be, and the day is lived out
accordingly. The second attitude, which owes something to the world of
accounting or other balances, assumes that there is the justice of percent-
ages in our lives. Respites will be balanced by hardships, snowlessness by
snow, ease by effort, and so on. The problem is that most people believe in
the first creed, but they tend to practice the second.

Another more intriguing snow-story involved an Anglican minister who
received a telephone call from one of his parishioners at 2:00 A.M. The
parishioner explained that he and his wife were at a party, had both drunk
a bit too much, were unwilling to risk a drive home in the snow, could
not summon a taxi and, therefore, wondered if he, the minister, could
in all charity come and drive them home. Since they were the minister's
close friends as well as his parishioners, he promptly agreed to fetch them.

After picking them up in downtown Pittsburgh, the minister proceeded to drive them home via the Boulevard of the Allies. It just so happened that the Ringling Brothers Circus was packing up for departure that very night from a week of performances at the old circus site near Point Breeze. Trucks and tented wagons were moving in caravan on the Boulevard of the Allies in the darkness of the March thaw. Lumbering behind the last truck, linked trunk to tail, were half a dozen elephants. As the minister drove past the caravan, his semi-inebriated parishioners in the back seat looked out of the window and saw elephants. "Hugh," said the husband to the minister, "you're going to think I'm crazy, but I swear I see elephants out there." "Out where?" answered the minister, straight-faced. "Right out there in the middle of the Boulevard of the Allies. There must be one, two, three . . . There must be six elephants out there." "Well, I don't see any elephants," said the minister. "Come on, Hugh, there are honest-to-God elephants right where I'm pointing." "I hope they're not pink," said the minister. The silence that followed his remark lasted for the remainder of the trip home. An almost total abstemiousness characterized the social behavior of the two parishioners thereafter.

If elephants seem out of place in Pittsburgh, at 2:00 A.M. or otherwise, the panthers or mountain lions (there are four) that stand guard in bronze replica at the opposite ends of the bridge over Panther Hollow are not.

Panther Hollow Bridge, 1990.

Panthers in Pittsburgh? It seems preposterous at first hearing, but the fact of the matter is that mountain lions at one time were not uncommon in the foothills of the Appalachians. Whether they were called mountain lions or panthers is beside the point, but in an earlier age these animals were an indigenous Pennsylvania species. Now they survive only in sculpture, and the four sculptures are eye-catching, consciousness-heightening. Even when certain fraternity vandals desecrated the bronze panthers some years ago by spraying them flamingo pink, the panthers did not lose their aura of vigilance. (The sculptor carved and cast them on the prowl). The offending pink was ultimately removed, and the bronze finish restored, leaving one to wonder again at the once-upon-a-time presence of these big cats in the area and to wonder further about the cat-like sneakiness that prompts some American troglodytes to leave their signatures of paint upon outdoor art. Pittsburghers do not suffer as much as New Yorkers from these spray-can-assassins (the impulse is almost the same), but they do exist and, like arsonists, they are rarely caught.

The panthers are but four of the many examples of sculpture on the Pittsburgh scene. The University of Pittsburgh Press recently published a definitive catalogue of these local sculptures. Co-authored by Marilyn Evert and Vernon Gay, this catalogue made it nothing less than humbling to be introduced (or re-introduced) to a host of *objets d'art* that you had more or less taken for granted most of your life. The names of Saint-Gaudens, Derujinsky, Vittor and Burke appear from an older generation, and then there are the names of Damianos, Calder, Moore and Cantini from more recent times.

Unlike Washington, D.C., for example, which seems to have more than its share of militarists on display (mounted generals, each with his appointed halo of pigeons, are as bountiful as embassies there), Pittsburgh's various war memorials always seem to commemorate the peace for which battles were fought and good lives lost and not glorify the specific architects of the bloodletting. The World War I infantryman at Doughboy Square has a look of fatigue and abandonment about him that is almost tragic, and the four-faced memorial at the intersection of Aiken and Liberty Avenues (each face commemorates one of the four military services) is a memorial to loss and not the vanity of war.

More frequently remembered in statuary in the city are public servants like Bigelow and Magee or sports figures like Honus Wagner or Roberto Clemente or philanthropists like Carnegie, Westinghouse and Frick. There is even one poet—Robert Burns. He stands in his tam-o'shanter beside the

Phipps Conservatory, and the fact that he was a Scot and that many of the early entrepreneurs in the city were Scots (Carnegie, Pitcairn *et al.*) made it almost inevitable that the largess and ethnic pride of the latter would make possible the commemoration of the former.

Of course, Burns is only one of the ethnic "saints" so commemorated. There is Frank Vittor's conquistador-like sculpture of Christopher Columbus at the entrance to Schenley Park that was subvented by Pittsburghers of Italian origin. At the time of its placement, a jurist named Michael A. Musmanno, whose theatricality in public, in the considered judgment of many, often bordered on demagoguery, took umbrage at the suggestion of one scholar that it was entirely possible and even likely that Leif Ericson had reached North America long before Columbus entered the hemisphere. Musmanno was so incensed that he told the scholar to make a trip to Schenley Park so that he could discover the true discoverer of America. Even though the most unscholarly reading of Columbus' own accounts confirms that he never touched North America but docked at various islands in the Caribbean, Musmanno ranted on as if Columbus had planted the flag of Spain somewhere near McKeesport. The result was a standoff. Musmanno's chauvinism survived intact. The scholar persisted in his accurate dissent, and the statue remains to this day as a testament to the noble incongruities that are often created by the combustible mixture of sincerity and pride.

An interesting history attaches to the bronze plaque that perpetuates the memory of one William Flinn in the City-County Building. Flinn was a senator who was prominent in Pittsburgh's political life in the late 1880's. The plaque was commissioned by the Roosevelt Commemoration Association and presented to the city by Governor Gifford Pinchot in 1925. The sculptor was a Russian emigré named Gleb Derujinsky. Consider for a moment the human, political and geographical intricacies, both national and international, that made it possible for Russian-born Gleb Derujinsky to accept this commission. And you are more than casually acquainted with these intricacies because you met Derujinsky in Manhattan shortly before his death in the mid-seventies. Raised in the very palace of the Czar, Derujinsky was a man who actually knew Rasputin as he knew all the Romanovs. As an art student in St. Petersburg and later in Paris, he, together with Carl Milles of Sweden and Ivan Mestrovich of Yugoslavia, was a student of and strongly influenced by Rodin. Following the overthrow of the monarchy, Derujinsky lived for a time in Europe before he came to New York. There his career burgeoned to such an extent that he was chosen to do the tablet of William Flinn as he was later picked to make the marble sculpture of "Europa and the Bull" for the New York World's Fair in 1936 and to go on to fulfill numerous other secular and liturgical commissions. Every time you see the Flinn plaque in the City-County Building, you cannot help but think that it has its roots in Moscow and St. Petersburg.

There is one piece of functional sculpture that has a permanent place in the unwritten history of trysts and appointments in the city. Every city, to be sure, has a place where people meet, and it doesn't matter if you meet in front of, behind, beside, above, to the right or left of, near or, in this case, under it. The "under" in focus here is the small portion of corner sidewalk beneath Kaufmann's clock. The clock itself is a baroque timepiece that attaches to Kaufmann's department store at the corner of Fifth and Smithfield. It juts over the sidewalk, and the phrase "under Kaufmann's clock" is probably the most commonly used of all rendezvous-signoffs in the Pittsburgh lexicon.

Any consideration of sculpture, particularly examples of functional sculpture like a clock, eventually suggests the art that deals with the creation of space, *i.e.*, the hollowed-out sculpture that has the name of architecture. And any consideration of architecture leads not merely to

When the Trains Still Ran, Penn Station rotunda from the Greyhound Bus Station, 1984.

prolonged discussion of Pittsburgh's houses and buildings but, eventually and much more poetically, to the silence in certain public buildings when the individuals who populate them are for various reasons absent. Schools, for example. Walk into any Pittsburgh high school during the Christmas recess or during a summer vacation, and the sense of space that confronts you is overwhelming. The scrubbed floors glisten. The unpadlocked wall lockers in July are like ranks of toy soldiers (or real soldiers for that matter) at perpetual attention. The classrooms have an orderliness that seems, in the vocabulary of an earlier decade, almost spinsterish, and the cheddar-sharp smell of wax and disinfectant in the stairwells and lavatories has an institutional sameness that you have smelled in a military barracks or airports at dawn. Speaking of airports, the Greater Pittsburgh International Airport at one or two o'clock in the morning has the pure peace of abandonment. The ticket counters are dark. Unclaimed suitcases are reserved in locked cages for their eventual claimers. A security guard or two ambles past the similarly caged concessions. The television monitors announce neither arrivals nor departures.

Perhaps the most dramatic stillness is the one that exists in empty performance halls or stadia. In the Syria Mosque or Carnegie Music Hall or Heinz Hall you have only the company of empty seats. But the seats are only half empty. The ghosts of all those who have occupied them in years past or who will occupy them in years to come are omnipresent. The stage, like a temporarily deserted highway, is underpulsed with the potentiality of motion, of sound, of life. In Pitt Stadium or Three Rivers Stadium there is that same sense of potentiality and readiness. The playing fields are primed to assume the man-devised and man-controlled conflicts of baseball and football. You had a kindred feeling when you were in Madrid years earlier and walked with your son across the packed sand of the floor of the Plaza de Toros. Invisible events seemed to be happening, or re-happening. Invisible crowds were booing or applauding. You could almost hear trumpets.

The silence of absence. The silence of waiting. There is a connection. You used to believe that the best way to get "the feel" of a city was to travel around its neighborhoods, to be shown the sights, to take walking tours. Now you're convinced that the deeper rhythm of a place reveals itself when you are waiting, usually involuntarily, in circumstances where you have no alternative. You've felt this while you were waiting in line for tickets, waiting in traffic, waiting in the anterooms of dentists' and doctors' offices, waiting in hospitals, waiting in airports. In the beginning you admitted to a growing annoyance caused by the delay, by the circumstances, by the very nature of waiting. Since one of the failings of Western man is the inability to remain still and profit from it, you learned early on that you were truly a Western man. But slowly you started to learn what all waiters learn. You stopped thinking "straight ahead" and began to think circumstantially. In ticket queues, for instance, you eventually turned and started to talk to the person in front of you or behind you. You learned what solidarity meant. You let the world go by. You lost yourself in trivia and in the process discovered in the anonymity of the queue itself a person inside of you that you forgot was there. And that someone was the same someone who was waiting to be discovered inside of everyone.

In traffic jams you realized more than once how much a modern city is at the mercy of machinery, and how much machinery is at the mercy of the most rudimentary laws of physics. Henry Adams was right when he wrote that the dynamo was at the core of industrial democracies. Under various identities it hums under automobile hoods as it does with different kinds of power in aircraft, in the basements of houses and apartment buildings, in factories and in the whole chromatic scale of our industry. Dependent upon that power in ways that we are less and less anxious to admit, we hew to its rhythms. In traffic jams it means that we wait. And we wait. And we wait. And while we wait, we learn why disagreements, conflicts and even wars can be spawned when the dynamo is threatened by any interdiction of its necessary food—capital and fuel. And then we start to ask ourselves if our dependence is not really a form of servitude. Robert Lowell put it more succinctly and memorably in a prophetic poem of his called "For the Union Dead" when, while he was describing traffic in downtown Boston, he concluded, "A savage servility slides by on grease."

As one of the doleful seated and waiting to be treated and hopefully solved by novocaine, by drill, by stethoscope, by thermometer, by blood-test, by prescription, by hypodermic or by the intelligent negligence that also has a place in the mystery of healing, you've known what another form of genuine dependence means. While waiting, you perused magazines that were rarely less than six months old, paged through albums that revealed the glories of Switzerland or French Impressionism, or you just studied your fellow waiters, who were dittoing your mannerisms, gesture by gesture. In the waiting rooms of hospitals you've known what it means to be at the total mercy of news of birth or death—first breath, final breath. You've known the utter helplessness of what it is to wait in such circumstances, and always the tigers of your imagination defeat the domesticated dog of your mind with visions of the worst that are beyond denial because they are, until a contradicting fact proves otherwise, entirely possible. You've thought of all you've done wrong or right. You've discovered the quiet question that is God, and you've known a new base at the core of your personality that the necessity of waiting mysteriously created in you. When you are in motion, you discover and define and pursue the individual you are. In the act of waiting, you come upon the person within you that is identical in everyone who exists or who has ever existed or will exist, and you understand at that instant what it means to be one and many at the same time.

Living with rivers breeds a different kind of resignation. After all, being built at the very vortex of rivers, Pittsburgh has the rhythm of rivers in its personality. Unlike seas or oceans, which are like nouns in their stationary size and presence, rivers seem to qualify more as verbs. They are destined to flow or die. When you drive alongside the Allegheny or the Monongahela or the Ohio, you feel the difference between car-time and river-time. The rivers pulse like blood at a specific speed and in a channeled course. They have maintained this tempo since they first flowed through uninhabited shores not yet known as Pennsylvania, through the era of the French and Indian Wars, through the age of the first factories and mills. Their banks have changed or been changed. Their bottoms, if dredged, would yield everything from sunken barges to cars to coffee cans to coins to human bones. Their force has been only slightly affected by locks and man-made sluices. But the pulse of their relentless motion has remained.

In recent Pittsburgh history there have been attempts, occasionally successful, to use the rivers for purposes other than those related to industry, sanitation or sewage. Sternwheelers have been introduced as tourist attractions as well as floating sites for private or corporate parties. There are motor boats on the rivers now and frequently they are towing water-skiers. One college president made a serious attempt to introduce varsity rowing and sculling contests on the rivers, but the attempt only proved that Pittsburgh and its rivers were not like Philadelphia and the Schuylkill in this one regard. But for years the American Wind Symphony Orchestra has used the rivers as highways for its floating stage—a Louis Kahn-designed barge from whose deck conductor and founder Robert Boudreau presents music by new composers performed by young musicians from all over the United States and abroad who have worked diligently to be part of the experience of bringing concerts to residents of Tarentum and other river towns.

Being a river-metropolis prevents Pittsburgh from being landlocked. True, Pittsburgh does not have the blue vistas that being located by an ocean or a great lake provides. But Pittsburghers know that their rivers are tributaries to the mid-country artery of the Mississippi whose destiny is to become part of the sea. By becoming aware of a river you become attuned to the rhythm of water on the move between meandering banks and flowing, always flowing to destinations that have been the same since the age of the great glaciers. If you watch a river from one of its banks, you almost feel whatever the myth of history is supposed to mean. You do not feel that by looking down at a river from a bridge (there are alleged to be more than eight hundred bridges in Allegheny County alone so that there are a lot of bridges from which one can look down). Seen from above, a river seems to draw you into itself, and you feel an atavistic fear that is akin to the fear that many feel when they look down at a sidewalk from the top floor of a skyscraper or when they peer into the eye of a volcano from an overpassing plane or even when they look into the dark at the bottom of a well.

Allegheny Spring, 2001.

But when a river is observed from the safe perch of a riverbank, it almost defines what natural freedom is and what natural force means. If what Heraklitos wrote is true, namely, that no man steps in the same river twice, then it is worth noting in passing that the river symbolized for him exactly what it symbolized for Mark Twain, Hart Crane and Thomas Wolfe—time itself. It mocks those minuscule toys we tell time with on our wrists or in our cars or on the walls or mantels of our homes. The river seems to tell time as time measures itself. And a city that has three rivers in its very anatomy is constantly reminded of that whether it wants to be reminded of that or not. It makes Pittsburghers keep in mind their transience, their scale, their mortality.

Once you touch upon mortality, you soon reach a point when you begin to talk about death. Death is linked to burial, and the burial customs in Pittsburgh are a microcosm of burial customs throughout the United States and have a sociological dimension that is often overlooked. As is true in most of the nation, the custom of "laying out" the dead in the very houses in which they spent most of their lives has given way to "viewing in" and burial from funeral homes. The names of funeral directors like Samson, Freyvogel, Blank, McCabe and Beinhauer are almost household words to most Pittsburghers. All of these men and their establishments attract a following of their own, and the same seems to be true of the hundreds of other directors (no longer undertakers) in the city. Frequently these followings are defined along lines of social status (or social pretension), religion, race or habit. For a person to be Samsonized seems to imply a certain aristocratic attainment. Catholics bury Catholics. Blacks bury blacks. Jews bury Jews. It seems that those people who have a strong ethnic orientation tend to choose funeral directors of a similar ethnic bent, and if the ethnically acceptable mortician does not in fact exist, then someone else who has served that role for reasons known only to the particular ethnic group in question is accepted for the job.

This creates a fascinating bit of Americana. However democratic or catholic a person was or strove to be during his lifetime, he or she is remanded to the inclinations and biases of the tribe in death. What Alexis de Tocqueville would have made of this phenomenon is open to finite speculation, but it raises questions about the behavior of Americans when it comes to last rites. Pluralism yields to tribalism, and the dead populate the city's cemeteries according to birthrights, customs, confessional ties and ceremonies that they, during their lives, may have taken lightly or even rejected. While some burials may be fitting and proper, others might easily qualify as the living's last effort to set things right by *their* standards or even as a last revenge.

Pittsburgh continues to be a city of neighborhoods: Squirrel Hill, Shadyside, Point Breeze, Morningside, Lawrenceville, Bloomfield, Hazelwood, Oakland, East Liberty and so on. It is apparent to most demographers of the local scene that the residents of these neighborhoods differ from those residents in neighborhoods that ring the city. Reflecting a national trend, young families for several decades now have moved and continue to move into the suburbs for a variety of reasons, i.e., schools, newer housing, bias, social or economic consanguinity.

The difference between the in-towners and suburbanites manifests itself not only in age and family orientation but also in economics. The owner of one supermarket in Mt. Lebanon, which is certainly typical in this connection, remarked that his larger, more streamlined store in Shadyside actually did less business per week than his smaller Food Gallery in the suburbs. "More people actually buy in Shadyside," he continued, "but they buy less. They buy for light housekeeping, and they also buy less because they tend to eat out a lot. Singles, divorced men and women, yuppies. . . . Out here in the suburbs it's nothing for the mother of a family to have a shopping bill of $100 or $150 a week, and that's on a regular and even a growing basis."

To say that the inner city has been left to singles of all descriptions or to apartment dwellers or the poor is to over-simplify. But there is a definite truth to the fact that the new base for large numbers of younger families is not in the city itself but around it. You detect it in the city parishes that have been steadily losing parishioners for the past two or three decades and whose remaining parishioners are in middle age or beyond. You detect it in the shutting down of neighborhood stores in the city that survived from generation to generation on family business. You find it in the desertedness of Schenley Park when the universities are not in session. How or when these patterns will change is a favorite form of prognostication when city planners convene, but no one really knows the answer. However, the ferment and the transition (if indeed it is a transition) create an ideal atmosphere for a brief consideration of the idea of progress. What, for instance, is true progress in Pittsburgh or in any city?

It is certainly something that goes beyond the shifts and ebbs of population patterns. Flaubert, more a cynic than a utopian with regard to the idea of progress, once wrote that unless progress was moral it was not truly progress. If we accept Flaubert's canon as a working hypothesis, we can readily conclude that progress must be related to quality if it is to be related to anything at all. In the same sense in which a good life is more humanly worthwhile than one that is merely long, so progressive cities should be concerned with what is truly good rather than be distracted by matters of secondary or tertiary importance. If, for example, something is destroyed in a city to make room for something else, it should be expected that its replacement will be better or at least as good. If there is a decrease in quality, the result is regress, not progress.

In this sense what often is castigated as nostalgia (parts of this memoir may even be regarded so) in certain Pittsburgh quarters is not nostalgia at all but a memory of a presence of quality in architecture, in road patterns, in social decorum, in public speech and in athletics that is often dismissed out of hand by those to whom progress is synonymous with the merely new. Such "progressives," it is hoped, are not the wave of the future. Pittsburgh's future will be served best by those who believe that what is new is not desirable if it is inferior to what it is supposed to replace. If replacement for replacement's sake becomes the order of the day, we face a predictable decline into banality that will sap all other efforts to create quality in our lives. "Built-in obsolescence" and the creation of "throwaways" or "discardables" are not ideals upon which qualitative civic life can be based. Thus far, with only a few exceptions, Pittsburgh has been spared cut-rate decisions regarding its future. It has had men who are wise enough to know that cheap solutions to expensive problems are not solutions at all and that cities that pursue such solutions are contributing to their own demise.

You remember something that N. Scott Momaday evoked when he wrote that a man in his lifetime once "ought to give himself up to a particular landscape in his experience; to look at it from as many angles as he can, to wonder upon it, to dwell upon it." It suddenly occurs to you that for many years you have looked at and, in an indescribable way, loved Pittsburgh in this spirit during your life. Away from it, you feel essentially alien, no matter where you are. Even in the south of France, which has a climate, a pace, a cuisine, a balance of work and leisure that attract you as nothing in Pittsburgh possibly can, you reach a point when you simply want to come home in order to feel at home—a mood you have never come close to approximating anywhere else. True, you remember hearing an exiled Czech writer who claimed that a man is not fully human until he achieves a state of being resident nowhere, thus making him truly a citizen of the world. And you recall what Timmerman said after he was deported from Argentina: "I am more at home in subjects now, not countries." But you could not help but note that these comments were made by men who actually were refugees and that such statements could readily be understood as the credos of intelligent men in such transient circumstances. You even had the suspicion that each of the statements smacked of rationalization.

Addresses and orientations may change, but the fact of the matter is that no one is from everywhere. Each of us is from somewhere, and if that somewhere remains accessible to you and if you stay there by choice, then to call it anything else but home is folly. You draw a certain strength from your residence there. You are part of the whole.

When asked why you stay in Pittsburgh, you always feel that you cannot give a specific reason. Like being asked why you chose your profession or married the person who is your wife, the answer and the question as well become bogged down in the mystery of life itself. You invariably offer the usual lame explanations, i.e., it's where you earn your living, where your family is, where you like the change of seasons and so forth. But you know in your heart that these are not reasons as much as they are facts, and you know as well that the final fact is that you can give no reason. You are here because you could never discover what home meant anywhere else. True, history and upbringing and opportunity have something to do with your staying. But there is something more. You have an intimation of what this something is each time you visit the plot of graves in Calvary Cemetery where the deceased members of your family are buried; you understand what continuity means by experiencing the connection that those left alive always feel in the presence of the dead. Beyond all religious belief, beyond the ineluctable ties of blood, beyond all power but the power of love, you know that the remains of those who loved and raised you are there beneath your feet, and in the grip of the feelings generated by that remembrance you have shamelessly knelt and prayed on that grave-cluttered slope in tribute to those dear and definite few. You felt that America in miniature was condensed in the ten square yards of Pennsylvania soil that covered those few people who journeyed from Lebanon to Marseilles to Ellis Island to Pittsburgh in the first decade of the twentieth century, who lived and raised families, who died in this country of their choice and love and who live on in your annually growing affection for and admiration and memory of them and their achievement. It confers upon the city that was their home and is now yours more than a geographical importance. It makes it yours, makes it you, a part of you forever.

But family memories are only a few of the memories that your life to date in Pittsburgh has bequeathed to you. Like all memorabilia they focus themselves in your consciousness at random . . .

A debate is being held in the Pitt Student Union between a businessman and an English teacher. The businessman claims that a college should *train* its students for a life in business, should *mold* them so that, as *products* of the university, they can immediately become part of the work force. The English teacher tries doggedly to prove that a liberal education should train and mold no one but rather should educate everyone for nothing less than freedom. The business man, exasperated, retorts, "What good is a liberal education anyway? All it teaches you to do is think . . . ."

A mezzo soprano is rehearsing on the stage of the Carnegie Music Hall. She complains with some hauteur to the hall manager that the piano is unsatisfactory. The manager responds, "Rachmaninoff played on that piano, sister . . . ."

It is the last year of the war in Vietnam. At the air freight warehouse near the Greater Pittsburgh International Airport a slightly scuffed aluminum coffin is parked on a loading dock. The coffin is girdled by two enforcing straps, and there are some lines of militarily lean data stencilled on the sides. On the top line is a name, last name first, followed by the abbreviation for lieutenant and an eight-digit number. The loaders on the dock give the coffin a wide berth, placing other pieces of luggage and freight more than five yards from it. The coffin could not be more alone—a vigil unto itself, a solitude, a loss . . .

In July the soft weather passes easily through your house or through the open windows of your car. You and other Pittsburghers make room for the weather, taste it, welcome it and channel it from entry to exit. In January the houses resist the weather. The weather stays *without*. Pittsburghers are truly *housed* then. Even the drivers and passengers in cars proceed like the encabined. Their faces have the expression of soldiers who are doing their best to remain cowled against the elements . . .

You drive by Richardson's jail on Forbes Avenue. Many times you have shown the jail and the bridge-attached courthouse to visitors to the city. As much as you admired the architecture, you always had a problem separating function from form. Whatever its architectural excellences, the jail was still a jail. You feel the same discomfort as you drive by the rear gate of the jail. It is open. You see several prisoners working as trusties around a garbage truck. An armed guard stands on the dock. The prisoners and the guard have the same casual stance, the same bored expression that you have seen in the faces of people who habitually have to wait for trains or elevators. They all have the same institutional heaviness in the way they stand. The only difference is in the clothes they are wearing. Of course, there is another difference. The guard is holding a rifle. The guard cradles the rifle so casually that it has an un-rifle look . . .

It will appear as a small item in all the newspapers across the country. The item will begin by naming a bridgeworker who was trapped in the superstructure of the Oakland-to-South Side bridge as it was being prepared for demolition. His leg was crushed and locked between two girders. Rescuers who reached him found him dealing as well as he could with the unspeakable pain and the obvious impossibility of release. The rescuers gave him a cigarette, tried to comfort him, called for more help even though they knew it was hopeless. Finally, the bridgeworker asked for a surgical saw. When he received it, he amputated, without anaesthesia, his trapped leg and then directed the rescuers as they placed him on a stretcher and lowered him to the floor of the bridge . . .

You note the new additions to the Magee-Women's Hospital. For decades a doctor named Barone and his associates delivered thousands of infants there. Now such deliveries are annually balanced by an almost equivalent number of abortions. For a moment you put aside the political and moral considerations of the abortion issue and just consider these tiny deaths as deaths, thousands of deaths. And then you consider the curious irony that is created by the intensive efforts to prolong life through open-heart surgery (a discovery of the middle and late sixties) in various other Pittsburgh hospitals. In Allegheny General Hospital the number of such surgeries per year is estimated at 1,200; at St. Francis Hospital, 400, and so on . . .

Teresa Heinz, the Mozambique-born wife of Senator John Heinz of the philanthropic Heinz family, is speaking on behalf of Peace Links to a group of teachers and social workers. She speaks feelingly of her hope for her own sons in a future free of the nuclear nightmare and then relates as an aside how one of her sons, exasperated with politics, said to her and her husband, "You and Dad are of an older generation, and that's old. And you both have been married a long time, and that's old." He paused and then added with a grateful smile, "Keep it up." By the tone of affection in Mrs. Heinz's voice, you understand instantly why she is fighting for her own and, intended or not, for everyone's children . . .

When Fritzie Zivic dies, it revives a lot of talk of Pittsburgh's firm place in fistiana. Old timers remember Harry Greb and claim with some justification that he was probably the best fighter who ever lived. Then there was Billy Conn who almost dethroned the great Joe Louis in his prime. Conn still lives in Pittsburgh, unostentatiously ...

Since taking over the A. W. Mellon Educational and Charitable Trust, Theodore L. Hazlett has godfathered a variety of artistic activities in the city. Now, having been told that he has colonic cancer, he continues to see to the various organizations that depend on the lifeline of his support. On one of your last visits with him, you hear him say that he wants to travel to California and pan for gold. It's something he wants to do if only to have done it. Knowing what he must be dealing with, you cannot help but tell him that you really admire his spirit. "What else can I do?" he answers. "I just hope I never lose whatever courage I ..." He cannot finish the sentence ...

An Eastern Airlines pilot is telling you of the time he was piloting a chartered flight for the New York Jets. Prior to the flight, the pilot spoke to Joe Klecko, one of the Jets' most "physical" players. Klecko proceeded to tell the pilot about the Steeler teams, the great elevens that won four Superbowls and, together with the championship Pirates, made Pittsburgh the City of Champions in the late seventies and shortly thereafter. Klecko, speaking with an athlete's honesty, said that the Steelers were so intimidating in their prime that other teams in the league were genuinely reluctant to play them ...

The old Brass Rail is gone from Wood Street. When George Williams was its manager, the Brass Rail made the best hamburgers in Pittsburgh. Somehow the combination of fresh beef, sauteed onions and crisp pickles was beyond duplication. When a new ownership tried to cut corners, Williams resigned. Implored by the owners later to return and save the business, he refused. One betrayal of the public was enough ...

It is Thursday, April 17, 1986. Mary Pat Flaherty is working at her desk on the editorial floor of the *Pittsburgh Press*. She knows that the series that she co-researched and co-authored with Andrew Schneider ("The Challenge of a Miracle: Selling the Gift") is one of three finalists for a Pulitzer Prize. She also knows that Pittsburgh has not had a Pulitzer awardee since corncob-puffing Ray Sprigle of the *Post-Gazette* won the prize for an investigative piece on the Ku Klux Klan more than thirty years earlier. Even though the announcement is imminent, she tries her best not to think of it. When her telephone rings, she answers quickly but still hesitantly. A pause. Then a smile. Then a broader smile as she turns to the reporters near her and says, "We won! We won!" Shortly afterward there will be a celebration in the editorial room with champagne and banners. But for Mary Pat Flaherty nothing will ever dim the exact second when she picked up the phone and heard, well, what she heard. A week afterward when you congratulate *Press* Editor Angus McEachran on the Pulitzer, he smiles his all-in-a-day's-work smile and says with memorable nonchalance, "What award?"

The Duquesne Club could easily hold its own in comparison with any of the private "gentlemen's" clubs along London's Pall Mall. Having evolved out of its original exclusivities, it still draws a firm line between business and social etiquette. No business papers or other paraphernalia, for example, are permitted on tables during luncheon or dinner. Although it now has a competitor across town in the Rivers Club in Oxford Centre, it has history on its side to enforce its claim to primacy. With its private meeting parlors, its various dining rooms, its billiard tables, its sitting rooms where bespectacled lawyers and executives peruse the *Wall Street Journal*, its rest rooms with their black marble urinals, its carefully screened ports of entry, its in-house tickertapes of the Dow and other averages, its reputation of having the best cuisine in the city, the Duquesne Club is probably as well governed and appointed as any of its counterparts throughout the world . . .

The name of Isaly was and still is prominent in the history of ice cream in Pittsburgh. Reputed to be the creators of the Klondike (a sandwich-sized square of ice cream coated with milk chocolate), the Isaly family featured

Big Isaly's, 1976.

an ice cream cone ("the skycraper scoop") that lived up to its name. The ice cream was cone-shaped so that it matched in reverse the cone that held it. Decades back, any father's major treat was to drive his family to the Isaly plant on the Boulevard of the Allies for a round of cones. You particularly remember a flavor called rainbow . . .

Adolph W. Schmidt, who was one of Andrew W. Mellon's most dependable officers as well as a decisive force in Pittsburgh's first Renaissance and then concluded his public career as ambassador to Canada, sits in a spare office in the Oliver Building. As a favor to Paul Mellon, he is overseeing the final dissolution of the A. W. Mellon Educational and Charitable Trust, making terminal grants, closing out the portfolio. Looking at the Mellon Bank across Smithfield Street, he says with a smile, "When A. W. was alive, there were three of us who took care of the bank's entire portfolio. Now it takes more than thirty floors of offices. It's another world. The economics I practiced, well, it's another world . . ."

Like most American cities, Pittsburgh has a pornographic side. It is of minor league proportions compared to Manhattan or Los Angeles. It amounts to the usual "adult" bookstores, parlors for "massage" and a dying theater or two trying to survive on quadruple X features. Somehow in every city the outward manifestations of pornography share identical uniforms: blatant yellow signs on which black and vermilion headlines broadcast the sexual ultimate. Their purpose is to shrink the public's attention from man to maleness to genitalia—from woman to femaleness to genitalia. The progression is from the unique to the generically the same. In this regard Helen Bevington's axiom is beyond improvement: "When you have nothing else to offer the public, show them your pudenda . . ."

Considered once the gateway to the West when the West was considered not much farther than the Pennsylvania-Ohio border, Pittsburgh still retains a kind of main-line axis or centrality that should keep it from ever becoming a wayside city. South-to-north, coast-to-coast as well as Chicago-New York flights frequently stop en route. Indeed, the nub of the country's most profitable airline, USAir, though administratively based in Washington, has its operational base in Pittsburgh, and a good many of its national flights originate or terminate here. As if to underscore the value of Pittsburgh's centrality, one traffic administrator, Anthony Sarkis of Colt International, declined to move to New York with his fellow administrative officers when the company was repositioned because he thought that Pittsburgh was more pivotal to all his relevant points of contact in the eastern United States. Using Pittsburgh as the center of a compass-drawn circle, he showed that the circle enclosed Atlanta, New York, Toronto, Chicago, Philadelphia, Washington and various other of the constellated cities within that circumference and, furthermore, that it would be less expensive to the company if he remained in Pittsburgh to conduct its traffic and transportation affairs. Because his case was irrefutable, he remained . . .

You stroll from the remodeled Schenley Hotel (you keep reminding yourself of that even though it is now the Pitt Student Union) to the Magee-Women's Hospital, a distance of less than six blocks. Gone is the Schenley Theater, the Park Schenley Restaurant, the Hungarian Garden, the few sit-down restaurants that once were landmarks. Quickie food-joints, catering to the student trade, have replaced them. Developers use words like "quantity," "turnover" and "low overhead." Strolling by them, you feel that you are in an alimentary penny arcade. Each hamburger dispensary is a tribute to food considered only as fuel. Only the brashness of a longstanding hotdog stand impresses you with its unhumble candor. For years the owner has bragged that his are the best hotdogs in the world. You've eaten them. They're every bit as good as the owner says they are . . .

Bridgeville is a community that borders Interstate-79 in Pittsburgh's southern quadrant. It has a small-town personality and a small-town stability to it. One day, while you were shopping there for fruit, you asked about a small factory tucked between an apartment building and assorted stores. You were curious to know what was manufactured there. "Submarines," answered an old Bridgevillian. You were speechless. Submarines in Bridgeville! The very thought seemed preposterous. Later you learned that the Bridgevillian had exaggerated somewhat. It was not submarines that were being manufactured in Bridgeville but optical components for the conning towers of submarines . . . .

A company known as TRACO, originally called Three Rivers Aluminum of the North Side, is now located in Cranberry Park and has a firm national reputation for making windows, industrial and residential. When the renovation of the Statue of Liberty was in process, TRACO was one of dozens of firms being considered to replace the bronze-framed windows in the statue's crown. TRACO was finally awarded the contract, and it proceeded to commission its craftsmen to obtain the exact measurements on site and then to hand-tool the idiosyncratic frames. The company's president, Robert Randall, surveying the gridiron-sized interiors of his fabrication plants near Mars and remembering his North Side beginnings, must have felt as if some dimension of his private American dream had been completely fulfilled at that moment . . .

There are other stories like this in the Horatio Alger tradition. In 1951 a mutual fund salesman named John Donahue made a single presentation to an official at the Pittsburgh National Bank to obtain backing for a money management idea. With the backing assured, Donahue and two friends from his high school days at Central Catholic created Federated Investors and, after a brief stay in East Liberty, moved to the Jenkins Arcade where they became the first street-floor brokerage firm in the city. To bring their idea to the attention of potential investors, they "knocked on a lot of doors" and handed out flyers and pamphlets. The idea took hold. Today Federated Investors, which is constructing its own headquarters building beside the equally new Vista International Hotel, is second only to Merrill Lynch as a money manager. The company's assets? Forty billion dollars . . .

When Philip Johnson's PPG Building was erected, it created much discussion about Pittsburgh as a Gothic city. In some ways the association is not outlandish. There are a number of French Gothic, English Gothic and pseudo-Gothic churches and like structures in Pittsburgh. The East Liberty Presbyterian Church, for example, could easily be at home in Southhampton or Hull, as could the United Presbyterian Church in Mt. Lebanon. The four-spired towers of both of these churches, which are smaller but duplicative of the National Cathedral in Washington, D.C., have a royal aloofness to them, as does, in its own neo-Gothic or mock-Gothic way, the PPG Building. But it would be farfetched to go much further in this consideration. Pittsburgh has a lot of English Tudor residential architecture, but it is not wise to generalize Tudorly along these lines any more than it is wise to generalize Gothically about an entire city because of a few spires.

The French Gothic tradition receives its due in churches like Calvary Episcopal and St. Paul's Cathedral. It was from the spire of the former that the antenna was mounted in 1920 from which the first nationwide election returns were broadcast by station KDKA. St. Paul's Cathedral celebrated its seventy-fifth anniversary recently and subsequently underwent a total refurbishing (the pews were sanded down to their ultimate oak and restained and polished), but for you it is still of special importance because it is where your mother and father were married in the mid-twenties. A jewel of a Gothic church is the First Baptist Church at the corner of Bayard and North Bellefield. Designed by Bertram Goodhue and constructed in 1912, it was awarded a first-place citation in that year as the best example of the fusion of French and English Gothic styles—a true Gothic revival. By a coincidence of geography, this church is one block away from the Heinz Memorial Chapel. A near replica of La Sainte Chapelle in Paris, the chapel, together with St. Paul's and the First Baptist Church, completes a memorable Gothic trio in the Oakland area . . .

The pastor of the First Lutheran Church on Grant Street, a small but welcome ecclesiastical presence between the Porter Building and other monoliths on the newly re-bricked and widest street in downtown Pittsburgh, is instructing a retarded boy on the eve of his First Communion. "George," asks the pastor, "do you believe in God?" "Oh yes, Father," answers George, "I believe in God, and I believe in His boy too. If I didn't believe in God and His boy, I don't know what I'd do." The pastor nods yes and then asks "And do you know what Holy Communion is, George?" "I know, Father," responds the boy, "It's when you go up to the front of the church, and the priest puts a cracker in your mouth, and then you walk around." The pastor nods yes again and smiles and keeps smiling . . .

The Chamber of Commerce sponsored a gala celebration of Pittsburgh's Rand McNally designation as America's most livable city in December of 1985. The locale was the David L. Lawrence Convention Center, and among the invited were Pittsburghers of origin or adoption who had gained national or international acclaim: Dr. Sidney Marland, director Milton Katselas, writer Abby Mann, actress Anne Jackson, fullback Franco Harris, broadcaster and actor Rege Cordic, ambassador Adolph W. Schmidt, who flinched noticeably when he was introduced as having concluded his public career as ambassador to China, and numerous others. Those who received the loudest applause when their names were called were from the University of Pittsburgh Medical School, Dr. Jonas Salk and Dr. Thomas Starzl—Salk for having discovered in Pittsburgh the vaccine that immunized the vaccinated from ever contracting polio, and Starzl for his work in organ transplantation. In the final analysis it was not the diplomats, thespians, athletes, educators, astronauts or broadcasters who struck the deepest notes of appreciation in the audience, but the healers . . .

During one of the post-season playoff games between the Pittsburgh Steelers and the Houston Oilers, no one seemed to notice that the names of the teams highlighted two of the major industries of the country. Fans were only concerned with the game itself since Houston-Pittsburgh games in that period proved to be the most vigorous and harshly contested games ever played. As it turned out, the Steelers won. At the final gun, one fan jumped from his seat to the playing field, ran after Houston Coach Bum

Phillips and snatched his Texas hat from atop his crew-cut. Years later when you chanced to meet Phillips over breakfast in Houston's Hobby Airport, you asked him if his hat were ever returned to him. "Oh yes," he said, "but I must have gotten more than three thousand letters, not just from Pittsburghers but from people all over Pennsylvania, and they all asked me not to judge Pittsburghers by the rudeness of one fan." He paused, chewed and swallowed a strip of bacon and added, "And I answered every one of those letters too." He smiled a coach's bedrock smile, remembering . . .

You are conversing over lunch with a professor of philosophy in Odessa, Texas. He tells you admiringly that he's heard that Pittsburgh has come a long way from what it was in the thirties and forties. He goes on to say that he respects Pittsburghers for having re-created the city from within, noting that most men rarely, if ever, understand the extent of the havoc they create until it is too late. "History," he says, "is a story of unintended consequences. And man's the problem, not lesser creation. The world can easily dispense with creatures of a higher order like us or like the lion without deleterious effects, but any disturbance of creation of a lower order like plankton, algae or some of the insects would have disastrous consequences for the whole of creation." The points he makes seem profound in themselves but without much connection to Pittsburgh. Later you will see the connection . . .

A young professional woman has moved from Washington, D.C., to Pittsburgh to work for Tito Capobianco at the Pittsburgh Opera. "Pittsburgh's a better place than Washington to work in," she says, "but Washington has better movies." She's correct. You remember that Pittsburgh at one time had a number of theaters that screened first-run foreign films on a regular basis. Now the Guild, the Forum and the Shadyside are gone, and their replacements (the Arcade before it burned down, the incipient Fulton, the reliable Squirrel Hill and too few others) have not really replaced them. The city is the loser. You've always believed that the growing cosmopolitanism of Pittsburgh's population requires cosmopolitan cultural opportunities. With the Pittsburgh Symphony, the Pittsburgh Opera, the Pittsburgh Public Theater, the International Poetry Forum and the annual Three Rivers Arts Festival (which has a foreign film festival built into its schedule), this cosmopolitanism is reinforced. But films, by far the most popular of the popular arts, need to have a firmer place in this constellation. Truly adult films by American and foreign producers need to counteract what one man exasperatedly condemned in your presence as the usual fare of "sharks, bees and disasters . . ."

You are showing the Russian poet Yevgeny Yevtushenko the obelisk-centered plaza of the PPG Building. (You have just finished discussing Shostakovich's "Songs of the Forest," one of your favorite of all of Shostakovich's compositions. Yevtushenko says that the sung poems in the piece are not good poetry, and that the whole piece was commissioned and written during the Stalin era to encourage reforestation in the Soviet Union). You tell Yevtushenko that plaza could make an ideal locale for a film by Antonioni. He brightens to the idea of film. "Wonderful place to make film, yes. The glass would reflect everybody different. A chase would be best here, no? Wonderful place even for poetry reading . . ."

The history of breweries in Pittsburgh is a history of taste. Beer metamorphosed from the early Irish flavors when local beers tasted like Guinness Stout to the lager beers of the Germans and, recently, in a more weight-conscious age to the "lites." The Pittsburgh Brewing Company must have done something right during its more than a century of existence since it is now the only surviving brewery in the area, exclusive of the Latrobe headquarters of Rolling Rock. Originally there were more than forty. Ranked as the ninth largest brewer in the United States, the Pittsburgh Brewing Company attracted the attention of an Australian millionaire named Alan Bond, who purchased it for almost thirty million dollars. He plans to leave the local management in place. This seems to be a wise decision since the company had net sales of forty-four million dollars in 1985, has a firm hold on 30% of the beer market in southwestern Pennsylvania and can offer overnight delivery of its beers to thirty states. If you have an interest in further facts about the company, you can visit its on-site museum where you can sample the various brews . . .

Pittsburgh is not only the home of the Clark bar, Zagnut and Crispy but also has contributed two dishes to the American cuisine. The first is the Devonshire sandwich, created by Frank Blandi in 1935 when he owned and managed the Stratford Club at Millvale and Center. Because the Stratford Club sounded "English" and because Devonshire Street (which also sounded "English") intersected Center near Millvale, he called the sandwich the Devonshire. It consists of a basic roux (a flour and milk mixture) intermingled with melted parmesan, mozzarella and any sharp cheese. The resulting sauce is then poured over chicken, turkey or crabmeat. If you ask Blandi today (he manages the restaurant at the Sheraton Hotel at Station Square) how best to serve the sauce, he will tell you that he prefers it "over fowl."

The second contribution by a Pittsburgher to the national cuisine is Crabmeat Hoelzel. As with the Devonshire, the secret is in the sauce (two-thirds of a cup of olive oil—*any* olive oil, one-third of a cup of tarragon vinegar, one tablespoon of salt and two tablespoons of coarse ground black pepper). Cooks at the Duquesne Club, where it was invented by a tycoon named Jack Hoelzel in Pittsburgh's heyday as an industrial center, will tell you that the sauce is at its best when it is served a day after it is made, which gives the ingredients a day to emulsify. It is then poured generously over cups of succulent crabmeat . . .

The cavernous David L. Lawrence Convention Center is being flanked by the new Vista International Hotel. With more than six hundred rooms envisioned for its guests, it promises to be Pittsburgh's most commodious hotel. Like its sister hotel in Washington, D.C., it will have an atrium but on a smaller scale. Years earlier the old Fort Pitt Hotel occupied the site, and there is some concern on the part of Vista officials to resuscitate some of the names of the Fort Pitt's banquet rooms and suites and reincarnate them if possible in the new hotel. People with an ear for history seem invariably concerned with letting the past bleed through into the present whenever the occasion presents itself. It strikes you as a good idea in the hotel business or whatever . . .

Concerning writers who lived or worked in Pittsburgh or simply passed through, you know along with everyone else that Gertrude Stein and Robinson Jeffers were born here (North Siders both) even though they ended in France and California respectively. You know that Willa Cather wrote here during her Friendship Avenue days and that Haniel Long had a long (pun more or less intended) residence on Beeler Street. In the last century Charles Dickens lectured here and departed, as his *American Notes* confirms, with something approaching contempt for the city and its then journalism; one newspaper Dickens identified laconically as the *Pittsburgh Sewer* and let the muckraking metaphor speak, or rather smell, for itself.

During the early days of this century it is reported that Carl Sandburg spent three days in Richardson's jail on a vagrancy charge during his hopping-the-freights period. Vladimir Mayakovsky read his poetry here in the twenties, and you conveyed that fact to his literary godson Yevtushenko when he read on the same stage forty years or so later. James Baldwin is said to have been born here as were W. D. Snodgrass (in Wilkinsburg, actually) and Annie Dillard, both Pulitzer Prize awardees, and Malcolm Cowley, the son of a Pittsburgh doctor. But Pittsburgh's literary profile is richer than a mere paragraph can suggest. It needs and deserves a separate book, and even now someone may be writing it . . .

No matter what writers saw when they were in Pittsburgh or what they wrote after they left it, it is impossible in any memoir or profile of the place to separate Pittsburgh from the hills that are part of its geography as well as its character. One North Carolinian, after spending a day in Pittsburgh, remarked to you that Pittsburgh was an interesting city but "y'all have all those heeeels." And hills there certainly are. Call them the foothills of the Appalachians, call them the typical topography of Western Pennsylvania, call them whatever you choose to call them, they nonetheless make Pittsburgh a city spared the endless horizons of Indiana or Texas or eastern South Dakota or the symmetrical city blocks of Phoenix or large hunks of Detroit. And they also give it what flatness cannot give. They give it diversity and, above all, the pedestrian difficulty that encourages vigor.

Duquesne University, which can only be reached by climbing the bluff on which it sits from one direction or another, could easily advertise the fact that it has a student body and a faculty with the strongest hips and legs in the community. This is because of the necessity of students and faculty alike to walk down and trudge up and then walk down again and trudge up again the inclines and the declivities that are part of its campus. Duquesne could also advertise many other things, i.e., that it has graduated the majority of judges in Allegheny County, that its own student body voluntarily helped it through a fiscal crisis in the sixties while other student bodies were turning their campuses into battlegrounds, that it has the best resources in the country for the study of existential phenomenology. In this regard there was a demonstration in the sixties when it was rumored that the administration of the college was threatening to excise existential phenomenology from the curriculum. The rumor had no basis in fact, but some students and some faculty members took to the then constricted campus streets with placards. The student newspaper, which has always had a satiric side, pictured a lonesome graduate student bearing a large placard which read SAVE PHENOMENOLOGICAL EXISTENTIALISM. Also in the same cartoon was a Pittsburgher who was offering the graduate student some coins and saying, "Save her if you can."

Another anecdote is related to the hills in Duquesne's daily life and to the wry realism of its students. Some years ago the Dean of the School of Business Administration, who later went on to be the President of the Catholic University of America, had a nine o'clock class in Canevin Hall on the bluff that he had to reach from his office in the now defunct Fitzsimmons Building downtown. He trudged the distance with the discipline of a Marine and was habitually there on the very stroke of nine. One

Wednesday he arrived early and realized that he had forgotten to mimeograph certain papers for his students. Leaving his hat and coat on the lectern, he marched back downtown, hiked back up after mimeographing the papers and arrived at twelve past nine. The classroom was empty, the students having availed themselves of a university rule that authorized dismissal of a class if the instructor were ten minutes late. The Dean was furious. When the class next met, he said, "Gentlemen, I was here last Wednesday before nine o'clock. I returned to my office to pick up some papers for you that I had forgotten. You certainly saw my hat and coat on the lectern. That should have told you that I was here. You could have waited. Gentlemen, from now on be advised that when my hat and coat are here, I'm here!" When the Dean next came to class, he saw only a hat and coat at every desk . . .

Idiosyncratic behavior may be as original as the aforementioned, or it simply may be symptomatic, perplexing or just plain intriguing. How many cities besides Pittsburgh have a fixed point where Fifth Avenue intersects Sixth Avenue or at least an extension of Sixth Avenue? How many restaurants serve a deliciously prepared fish called Virginia Spots? Pittsburgh restaurants do. What are Virginia Spots, and where are they caught? Research will confirm for you that no such fish exists and that Virginia Spots are a certain genus of bass. Where did the name come from? You have yet to discover the answer.

How many cities besides Pittsburgh have the crazy birds of the Liberty Bridge? These birds, perhaps wrens or sparrows, roost on the underpinnings of the bridge, but something about the bridge itself or the air currents around it or some force known only to these birds or to ornithologists drives them skyward in flocks above the bridge floor, and they soar and veer and then dive by the fifties or the hundreds down under the bridge and up again, clouding up like blown ashes from a campfire or zig-zagging like a tangle of Spads and Fokkers and Sopwith Camels in a free-for-all when it was every man for himself in a dogfight. It is fascinating to watch these birds for hours at a time if you have the time. They seem driven by some berserk fury to wheel and zoom and climb as if their very lives depended upon it. And they never seem to tire. The fiercer the wind or the more turbulent the weather, the more furiously do the birds fly and the more incredible their convolutions. Yet, oddly, they do not collide, nor do they strike the bridge floor nor any of the automobiles thereon. They confine their maneuvers to the air, and the drama of their Stuka dives and Immelmanns is one of Pittsburgh's permanent inexplicables.

Now a few other images and names at random—the sight of the flooding Monongahela, its high brown waters like a chill and killing sauce over the parking wharves, its flotsam of branches and an occasional crate punctuating the downstream current and reminding you of Katherine Kressman Taylor's *Diary of Florence in Flood* when she wrote of awakening on November 4, 1966 to see the swollen Arno carrying toys, trees, oil drums and chairs in its pounding rush through the city of Florence together with a single drowned cow that floated in a whirlpool around one of the bridge pilings and just kept circling and circling there—Roberto Clemente in the act of exercising his neck as if to demonstrate to the neck that it was after all *his* neck and that he wanted and needed it as limber as possible. You remember that image in game after game. The day after Clemente was killed on January 1, 1972 in an airplane crash off the coast of Puerto Rico, the Alcoa digital sign atop Mt. Washington flashed out a simple blue epitaph, *"Adiós, Roberto"*—For decades the Connelley Skill Learning Center, which is one of the few buildings that survived the renovation of the Hill, has trained boys of high school age in carpentry, masonry and other crafts. They literally learn by doing. To learn to lay brick, for example, the apprentices actually build miniature walls in the masonry workshops.

The St. Patrick's Day Parade passes the reviewing stand in front of the City County Building. The old timers as well as the new timers cannot help but note an ethnic changing of the guard. Mayor Richard S. Caliguiri and Bishop Anthony J. Bevilacqua are waving and smiling as Irishly as possible—Princess Grace of Monaco is standing at the window of the Le Mont Restaurant at night. She is peering out at the spread of lights and shapes on the near and far side of the river beneath Mt. Washington. For a moment, she says, she is reminded of how Monte Carlo looks at night when viewed from almost any spot on the Grande Corniche. The discovery of such a sight in Pittsburgh makes her smile. Though a Philadelphian by birth, she has never been to the city before.

Adlai Stevenson is campaigning as the Democratic presidential candidate in the Urban Room of the William Penn Hotel (now the Westin William Penn). Stevenson is obviously unsure of the identities of those assembled to hear him. Are they party workers, Notre Dame alumni, Knights of Columbus, independents? Nobody seems to know. Adroitly Stevenson begins his remarks by quoting a story about Al Smith when he went to speak to the prisoners at Sing Sing during *his* presidential campaign. Smith, said Stevenson, addressed the prisoners by saying, "My fellow Democrats." He thought instantly that this was in need of revision, so he added prudently, "My fellow Americans." Somehow the *double entendre* of his original opening seemed to be compounded rather than erased. At last he said, "Well, I'm just glad to see you all here." Having cauterized the awkwardness of the situation, Stevenson then went on with his speech. This was during the second of his two campaigns, and he spoke like a man who knew he was going to lose but whose faith in his gradually weakening cause would be enough to carry him through the election. He lost, and it did.

Night in Highland Park. From their pits in the zoo you can hear the lions' gulping cough that is frequently misidentified as a roar. It's a resonant cough, not a roar, but nonetheless the sound of lions in a Pittsburgh park is something to ponder on a summer night.

Evening on Mt. Washington. The Alcoa sign is flashing a not too subtle Promo out over the city: SEE VAN GOGH SHOW. You wonder what Vincent would think if he were alive to see it—Francoise Gilot, once Pablo Picasso's companion-artist and now Mrs. Jonas Salk, walks into the Carnegie Library where a young secretary is reading her *Life with Picasso*. It is pure coincidence. The girl does not know that the author of the very book she is reading is standing in front of her—Melvyn Douglas is strolling along Fifth Avenue, the script of Archibald MacLeish's *The Great American Fourth of July Parade* under his arm. He is in Pittsburgh to portray Thomas Jefferson in that play opposite George Grizzard's John Adams. While he walks, he is remembering how he used to visit Pittsburgh when he was stationed at Indiantown Gap during the Second World War. He somehow creates his own ambience as he walks, and he seems totally ready for death. Like Edward G. Robinson he has become with every part a better actor as he's grown older—A woman in a large hat has just asked a docent in Carnegie Institute where she can see the permanent collection. The docent senses that she has seen the woman somewhere before, but she is unable to place her. Still wondering, she leads her to the gallery and realizes as she goes that the woman in the large hat is Katharine Hepburn—The clean dazzle of Kennywood Park. Most Pittsburghers don't know that the park was built in the first place by the Mellons as a recreational facility for their employees—The bridges known as the Three Sisters across the Allegheny rhyme with one another. Some nights when you look at them illuminated, you have the feeling that you are looking down the Rhine or the Seine—The incongruity of the new McDonald's in the very middle of the Strip astounds and confounds you. You wonder why anybody would want to eat McFood in the middle of all this bounty—The definite aroma of good perfume on the ground floors of Pittsburgh's three leading department stores, Kaufmann's, Gimbels and Joseph Home's, is tactical. You agree with the tactic. If you have to smell anything when you enter a department store, why not perfume?

How do you extract from this phantasmagoria what is unique about Pittsburgh? You think and think and think some more, and finally you conclude that Pittsburgh's distinctiveness grows from its resilience, its grit. At a time when the unemployment picture is still grave, when its basic industries are liquidating or retrenching and its newer industries are just beginning to establish themselves, when its inner city transportation plans are slowly being transformed—Pittsburgh still manages to be rated the most livable city in the United States. True, there is a taint of near despair in outlying boroughs like Aliquippa and Ambridge and Brad-

Kennywood Memories—Turning, 1988.

dock and Carnegie where the out-of-work steelworkers and their families are trying determinedly to make ends meet, but you feel that there is an underlying doggedness that needs only the spark of a rebirth to manifest itself. Migration is not an answer for these people because of family ties and because many of them feel they are too old (but not that old, really) to take a chance elsewhere even if they wanted to, and as Pittsburghers they don't want to. Who cares, they say, about the Sun Belt, about Denver, about California, about Dallas? Their neighborhoods in Carnegie and the South Side are maintained as well as pride and shrunken savings will permit, and there is a determination not to let the once crowded streets turn into slums. There is also a resilience that says hard times are a part of life and that there have been hard times before. It's the persistence and the forbearance and the endurance that are important. At a time when most Americans are identified as corporate gypsies or yuppies or believers in sideward or upward mobility, there is something to be said for the endurers. They are the Greek chorus in the Pittsburgh part of the American drama that holds the plot together.

Perhaps it is this resilience that may be at the core of Pittsburgh's existential character. Outsiders who came to Pittsburgh and attempted to change the city into their image of it invariably met the same fate. They stayed around for a few years and then were thrown to the peripheries by centrifugal force. One industrialist, for example, once threatened to bring workers from Germany to replace those he considered ne'er-do-wells in Braddock. The men of Braddock are still there, but the industrialist has since evaporated.

Existentially speaking, Pittsburgh seems to have a nature that is non-distortable. While some cities strive to be what they once were or what others think they should be, Pittsburgh is in conflict with no false images of itself. In short, it is not in competition with itself or with any shadows of itself. Los Angeles obeys an almost amoeboid principle of growth. New York is at the mercy of power plays and overpopulation, and you have the feeling that all of its celebrated endorsers who tell you with such smiles how much they "love New York" from airport posters across America are the same people who look over their shoulders when they return to their hotels or apartments after midnight. Miami is two cities at once, and Dallas abounds with instant neighborhoods. Pittsburgh seems to keep its character intact through phases of change. The façades are different, but the faces of people and things have an obdurate persistence about them. Overviewers tried to change East Liberty, and the results were lamentable, but even at this minute there are stirrings that betoken East Liberty's re-creation from within, storefront by storefront.

There was James Parton in the last century who described Pittsburgh as "hell with the lid off," and then there was Frank Lloyd Wright who, when asked by certain city fathers what could be done to make Pittsburgh more livable, responded with the famous cryptic and funereal, "Abandon it," but Pittsburgh has somehow refuted its condemners and transcended its own circumstances to become the metropolis it now is. The real character of the place, like the resilience of its native population, is constantly in the process of defining itself when tested by life's vagaries or by time itself. Each testing redefines it in the same way that suffering redefines and re-etches a human face without changing it. In this way Pittsburgh remains defiantly and stubbornly Pittsburgh.

Nevertheless, you cannot forget that Pittsburgh, like all other American cities, is not insulated from the ultimate atmosphere of our time—the nuclear age. The right-wing hawkers at the Greater Pittsburgh Airport (a new airport is underway even though there are political and other forces opposed to it) keep distributing their leaflets that advocate "nuking" the opposition. They proclaim to your face that their patriotism is the only patriotism there is. If nuclear madness has a name, they are it. As total

Second Avenue, Hazelwood, 1987.

and unthinking in their belief as Hare Krishnas or Moonies or other "true believers," they stand out like blatherskites of hatred amid largely and blessedly indifferent passengers who are heading for non-nuclear business appointments or vacations in Milwaukee or San Diego or Hawaii or the Cote d'Azur.

Still, the shadow of the bomb outspeaks its kookie proponents. You remember hearing a talk by a superannuated colonel in the sixties who claimed that the smallest bomb in the American or Russian arsenal would, if detonated at the point of Pittsburgh's Golden Triangle, leave a crater of approximately two hundred square miles and that the fallout would kill untold thousands to the south and east, depending upon how the wind would be blowing after impact. The specter of such destruction impelled many Pittsburghers to construct or refortify their backyard bomb shelters at the time. The specter slowly shrank, proving that fear and horror have their motivational limits. But the threat remains. Considering that the colonel's remarks were made in the nuclear equivalent of the Middle Ages (our bombs are "smarter" and more "surgical and sanitary" at present), you cannot help but wonder what size such a crater would be today, more than two decades after his prophecy. For starters you know that "the bomb" has one million times the power of the one dropped on Hiroshima, and everyone knows what happened there. Translated into the middle and late eighties, the devastation creates an unspeakable portrait of horror. A city that has been two centuries in the evolving would be turned into a scorch that would be as bare as a prairie swept by the mightiest of cyclones.

The mentalities of most city dwellers, Pittsburghers included, have been formed by the apocalypse. However unspeakable, it creates a fear, and that fear begets a response. That response, in civic and national terms, is defense. There is one school of thought that believes that our cities and country should be ringed with warheads, mimicking the atavism of the colonial settlers who surrounded their settlements with stockades. Old Fort Duquesne at the Point (later Fort Pitt) testifies to this habit of mind, and an intact ancestral relic still exists near Uniontown in George Washington's Fort Necessity. If you study the fort, you see a certain similarity between the pointed peaks of the stockade logs and the warhead tips of the upstanding rockets in our various defensive perimeters. The difference, of course, is in the "payload," but there is no denying that both the log and the rocket share the same defensive and deterrent function. It is as if history, from Cain's rock to the modern rocket, is repeating itself (as it invariably does) but at much higher stakes.

So, behind the protective palisade of Intercontintental Ballistic Missiles, Pittsburghers, like other Americans (and perhaps like other Russians), go on living their post-Hiroshima lives. They shop in Market Square, dine on the South Side or in Squirrel Hill, worship in church, synagogue and temple and play the state lottery. They no longer prepare for the worst and try not to think about it since the worst is beyond defense and even beyond imagining. They simply hope that the worst will not happen, basing their hope on the lowest common denominator of "mutually assured destruction" and the reasoned belief that destruction, mutually assured or not, is a fate that no government would invite or choose. Of course, this does not take insanity or rational stupidity or Poe's "impulse to the perverse" into account, and it is of such that tragedies are born. Like Sabatini's Scaramouche, the best posture for men and women in our time is to be "born with the gift of laughter and a sense that the world (is) mad." The result is that somewhere between hope and fear, Pittsburghers go on living out their lives with the gift of Scaramouche's laughter as their only human defense, and in this sense they are the same as everyone else at this moment on the face of the only earth we still have.

1992

The Pittsburgh that stays within us is never a finished portrait. Like human lives, which are in continual flux and never end when we think they should, cities are never in a finished state, and it is utopian to think that they ever will be. They are always being renewed, repaired, renaissanced, re-designed, re-renewed, re-repaired and so on indefinitely. Pittsburgh does not differ from other cities in this regard. One way it does differ, however, is that its renewals occur within fixed boundaries, unlike Detroit, for example, which is slowly but steadily recentering in the direction of Flint. The confluence of the Allegheny, Ohio and Monongahela Rivers and the contiguous real estate contained therein remain the unshiftable hub around and from which the city radiates. Within that centripetal hub, buildings are torn down and others rebuilt in their steads, structures renewed from within, streets and avenues and boulevards re-surfaced. Often as I walk or drive through the city and observe how the new has

Spring comes to Schenley Park, 1988.

replaced the old, I find myself wondering if I can remember what had been there. And more often than not I can't, or, if I can, the image comes to me like something in a dream, as if the previous reality had existed only in my mind—as indeed it did in part and, in my more lucid moments, as it still does.

Take Grant Street, for example. It has been re-surfaced with hand-set reddish-brown bricks, and it is punctuated at various points by island-dividers replete with trees and auxiliary landscaping. Looking at it, I try to recall the old Belgian block cobblestones, the trolley tracks, the floodwaters that crested there in the thirties. Finally, I simply resign myself to the present tense. It is still Grant Street after all but with a new and attractive face or re-face. Its history even permitted it to survive a well-intentioned but ill advised suggestion that it be renamed in memory of Pittsburgh's late mayor, Richard S. (for Sylvester) Caliguiri, who died in office on May 6, 1988 of amyloidosis.

A few more words about Mayor Caliguiri. An activist and a natural mingler who never cheapened the mayoralty or lost his dignity in public, he established and maintained a reputation as a man to whom the city had a personal—even a familial-significance. When it was rumored (and more than rumored) that the Pittsburgh Pirates would leave the city, the mayor led a coalition to keep the team "where it belonged." Also, like Fiorello LaGuardia, he often went where the trouble was—a train derailment, a toxic leak, whatever. When an oil spill occurred in the Allegheny River, the mayor was on site and on the telephone to speed the clean-up.

During the aforementioned oil spill the owner of an air-conditioning company hand-lettered a sign in front of his building on Banksville Road for the benefit of all drivers coming into downtown Pittsburgh from the South Hills: "All the oil you can drink." This kind of humor is not only characteristic of Pittsburghers when they are confronted with a non-lethal crisis, but it has been turned into a fine art by this air-conditioning company owner on repeated occasions. After a heartbreaking Steeler loss to the Houston Oilers (on a dubious call by a linesman), the signmaker had a single word for drivers to read the next morning. The word is commonly associated with toilets, but on that morning it captured everyone's sense of frustration and injustice. On another occasion there was a sign that left nothing to the parental imagination: "For Sale. One 14-year-old. Knows everything."

After having been diagnosed with amyloidosis, Mayor Caliguiri continued in active office until his death at his home on the evening of May

6, 1988. By coincidence this was the very day when Dr. John E. Murray was chosen as Duquesne University's first lay president. Within three years Murray would restore Duquesne to its traditional identity by having the wisdom to let the university "happen" rather than permit anyone to impose an individual or collective will upon it. He emphasized the primacy of teaching as the university's basic mission, bolstered library holdings, had the campus qualify as one of the safest in the United States while fostering an endowment in excess of $25,000,000. And he did this while following the Wilsonian example of teaching a course in contracts in the university's law school—a subject on which he is nationally regarded as an expert ("Murray on Contracts" was and is for many as definitive as "Goren on Bridge"). Comparisons were made between Murray and Robert Maynard Hutchins of the University of Chicago (both former law school deans who became university presidents), but Murray, though an admirer of Hutchins, kept his own counsel and direction and did not belabor the similarities.

The legacy of Mayor Caliguiri is generally regarded as having contributed significantly to the election of the present mayor, Sophie Masloff, but there was an artistic legacy as well. Robert Berks was commissioned to create a memorial sculpture of the late mayor. Although it was a matter of more than casual controversy at the time that a sculptor from some place other than Pittsburgh was chosen, Berks came through with a remarkable piece of work. (A different controversy arose when, for totally opposite reasons, Mark DiSuvero was commissioned to create a sculpture to be erected in Gateway Center. The commissioning drew such a crescendo of protest from amateurs and cognoscenti alike that the entire matter was permanently tabled). Unlike the huge head of John F. Kennedy that Berks sculpted for the main lobby of the Kennedy Center for the Performing Arts in Washington, the memorial to Mayor Caliguiri is of a standing figure. The pose is of a man in a semi-slouch, head slightly forward, face suggesting pensiveness and concern, a map of the city at his feet. Somehow the pose conveys a sense of the loneliness of office and simultaneously the burden and sadness of it. Many Pittsburghers look up rather furtively when they pass the statue near the main entrance of the City-County Building as if they do not want to be reminded of the saga of a courageous man who for months faced the inevitability of predicted death simply by being his gradually fading self before their very eyes until that final evening in May of 1988. All who look at the statue cannot help but be reminded of that.

Years later an equally popular political figure, Senator John Heinz, was killed when his private plane collided with a helicopter over a Philadelphia schoolyard. Heinz, whose familial legacy and personal interventions on behalf of his Pittsburgh constituency made his name a household word in the city, was perceived almost in eternal terms as an officeholder. His death seemed the ultimate absurdity. One was suddenly plunged into Camus' view of the universe where chance was king or into a memory of an Anglo-Saxon poem which says that men and women meet death in three ways only: age, disease or violence. It was the violence of Senator Heinz's death that lingered in the mind, the unspeakable image of a mid-air collision, of those final seconds. Later one saw the grief and bravery in the face of his widow, Teresa, as she supported and was supported by her sons at the funeral, and one knew instinctively that his legacy of public and charitable service would not die.

As mentioned, Mayor Caliguiri's leadership did much to keep the Pittsburgh Pirates in Pittsburgh and precipitated a revival of interest in the team and in baseball itself. Fanatical football fans, who claimed that Pittsburgh was at heart a football and not a baseball town, waited in vain for the Steelers to return to their Superbowl stature. It has yet to happen.

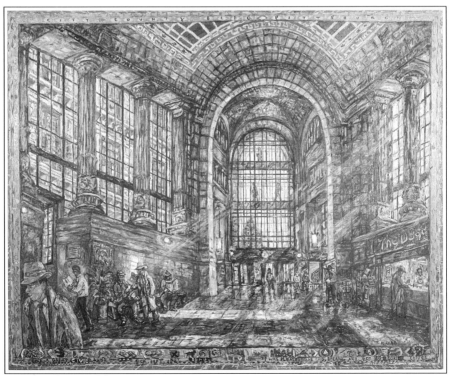

City-County Building, 1988.

Because such dreams of a renaissance of past glory die hard (if at all), there were recurring demands for the resignation of Chuck Noll during the late eighties. Noll, the deservedly heralded coach of the Superbowl years, was said to have "no imagination," of making his players conform to his system and not of changing the system to suit the talent of the players, of being an "emperor." One critic noted that too many professional football coaches were former linemen (as Noll was with the Cleveland Browns during his playing days) and that they thought like linemen when it came to offensive strategies, which meant that they thought defensively and conservatively by nature and training. "Once a lineman, always a lineman" was the common truism that circulated in the bars, hotel lounges, newspaper offices and living rooms of the city.

Noll eventually did resign, but the choice seemed to have been his exclusively. If it was, then it further testified to his magnanimous side since staying on in the face of mounting dissatisfaction would have placed his boss and friend, Dan Rooney, in the unenviable position of letting him go. Anyone who knows the fairmindedness of Dan Rooney realizes how odious an act that would have been for him.

Widely respected as a teacher of football fundamentals, Noll left a certain aristocratic and selfless standard as his legacy. Although some of his critics and former players accused him of a basic flintiness and lack of feeling, he nonetheless steadfastly refused to cash in on his position by involving himself in advertising endorsements and the like (compare Mike Ditka, for example). Noll left the perks to his players. That alone, regardless of the record of the Steelers in the seventies and eighties, gives him a stature and a certain statemanship that is not common among his many co-professionals. When his successor was chosen, Noll was asked if he had any advice for Bill Cowher (a native Pittsburgher, by the way). He demurred, adding modestly, "I just don't want to get in the way."

The sport that has come in to its own in Pittsburgh in the past five years is hockey—winning hockey, Stanley Cup hockey. I am not a true hockey fan inasmuch as I do not know the rules and subtleties of the game. As a boy I knew a player from the old Pittsburgh Hornets, but the Hornets never commanded the kind of frenzied support that one finds at the Civic Arena when the Penguins are in town. Like many Pittsburghers I was caught up in the saga of the 1991 end-of-season when the Penguins not only won their divisional championship but triumphed through the play-offs and earned the Stanley Cup. (The Stanley Cup in Pittsburgh? It seemed an oxymoron, but no longer). Even as I write, the Penguins have just been awarded their second consecutive Stanley Cup. They earned it by defeating Washington, New York, Boston and, finally, Chicago, despite the loss in whole or in part of some of their key players, including Mario Lemieux, during the play-offs themselves. Like 1991, the 1992 play-off series was a triumph of spirit as well as talent. And the crescendo with the Chicago Blackhawks resulted in a sweep of the series by the Penguins, giving them a record-tying eleven game winning streak to conclude the post-season.

The day after the Penguins won the divisional championship in Detroit in 1991, I happened to be booked on the same return-flight with the team. When I observed them in the waiting lounge, they gave me the impression that they didn't quite know how to handle their happiness. They were all wearing suits and ties even though they did not look comfortable in suits and ties—like high school or college boys fulfilling a requirement. Each one had a visible battle-wound—a fresh forehead nick, an absent incisor or two, a scrape on the cheek, a swollen lip. Coach Bob Johnson, who would die quietly and bravely from a brain tumor a few months later, was accepting congratulations and talking with his players, one at a time. The great Lemieux showed the confident modesty of a born champion.

Watching Lemieux on the ice makes one realize that there is Lemieux at one level and then there is everybody else. He seems to have the gift of seeing the game simultaneously at ice-level and also from somewhere above the action. His reputation among Canadians was brought home to me once when I was saying goodbye to the distinguished Quebecois poet Gaston Miron at the Greater Pittsburgh International Airport. After he boarded his plane, I stood at the gate beside a man I did not know. We exchanged a word or two. He told me he was a Canadian who lived in Pittsburgh and added, "You have brought our best to the city." I thought he was talking of Miron. I agreed, saying that Miron was probably the finest poet in the French-speaking world at the moment. The man was puzzled. He waited a moment and said, "I was speaking of Mario Lemieux."

Back to the Pirates. At the onset I must confess to a visceral and incurable allegiance to the Pirates—the allegiance of the lover, fraught with everything from disgust to anger to ecstasy but always there. It was there during the Kiner and Hank Greenberg years, the era of Branch Rickey and Joe L. Brown, the Pirates-Yankees World Series of 1960 so deliciously keened over by James Reston in a *New York Times* editorial entitled "O Cruel and Fateful Acts of Piracy," the Baltimore series of 1971 and then Baltimore Segundo in 1979, the death of Roberto Clemente, the drug trials, the slow re-building under Syd Thrift, Larry Doughty and Mark Sauer, the steadiness of Jim Leyland.

Clemente deserves special mention. Memories rise and lap and over-lap—the matador stance at the plate and in the field, the special hauteur that only the Latin Americans can muster, the public face and demeanor that (for me) seemed reminiscent of a similar decorum in Joe DiMaggio both on and off the field, the constant concern, as was the case with DiMaggio, to be sartorially flawless. Watching Clemente play right field in Forbes Field and later in Three Rivers Stadium was as electric as watching him bat. Batting, Clemente hit off his front or left foot, breaking the basic rule that a batter's power came when he anchored his strength on his back foot. Instructors simply said that Clemente was an exception, and, judging from the results and taking due notice of his 3,000 hits, they all agreed that it was wise to have left his stance to its unorthodoxy. As a fielder, Clemente did not merely play right field; he owned, he diagrammed, he wrote the book on right field. Whether he was playing the bounces when the ball ricocheted off the treacherous angles of the right field corner of Forbes Field (Pete Reiser of the old Brooklyn Dodgers once knocked himself out by slamming into one of the abutments there) or, on occasion, when he actually threw out from the deepest part of right-center field a runner attempting to score from third after the catch, Clemente fielded and threw like a master. His unorthodoxy frequently included throwing behind the runner as he rounded first or second (a no-no for most other fielders), but many was the runner who saw that Clemente's throw actually beat him to the base that he had rashly passed and tried too late to re-touch.

Clemente's death was a genuine period of mourning in Pittsburgh. He had just assumed the mantle of a superstar after an outstanding season (3,000 base hits). Having felt that he had been underestimated and under-praised (he was correct) for years, he nonetheless did not batten on the publicity when he returned to Puerto Rico. Instead he used his fame to focus attention on earthquake victims in Nicaragua. He even rented a plane and stored it with supplies and promised that he would personally deliver them to the Nicaraguans. He appeared on television nightly, exhorting his fellow islanders to join him in the effort. Finally, he boarded the improperly loaded plane and headed for Managua. After take-off, the load shifted. The pilot attempted to return to San Juan but never made it. When it was announced that Clemente had perished in the crash, Willie Stargell and other team-mates wept openly. Manny Sanguillen even volunteered to dive and retrieve Clemente's body. I followed the Latino developments closely because I happened to be in Mexico at the time. His death was like the death of a great matador; it cast a pall over the country. Three days after the crash one newspaper headline, with a certain reverence, read simply: *No se encontró . . .* He has not been found.

The re-building of the Pirates went on for most of the seventies. It was not enough to attempt to find another right fielder; the entire chemistry of the team had to be re-created. Chuck Tanner finally found the right mix in 1979, and the Pirates faced the Orioles for the second time in that decade. It also marked the first time I saw a World Series game in person, and I did so in the best way possible—with my 13-year old son. Neither of us will ever forget the scorn with which Jim Rooker treated Earl Weaver's peevishness at the beginning of that pivotal fifth game. The Pirates were at that point losing the series, three games to one. Weaver complained because Rooker had a white bandage on his wrist, and the umpires ordered Rooker to remove it so that it would not be a distraction to the Baltimore batters. Rooker, who had publicly stated that the Orioles were vulnerable to lefthanded pitching, complied by removing the offending bandage and flinging it into the Baltimore dugout. Rooker then proceeded to prove his announced theory by muting Baltimore's formidable hitters until the late innings when he had to be relieved (with the Pirates in the lead). The winner of the next game was John Candelaria, another lefthander. Then Grant Jackson, a lefthanded relief pitcher, won the seventh game, thus vindicating Rooker.

If pitching was decisive in the 1979 series, it continued to be decisive through the eighties when the Pirates were re-tooling. Finally, at the beginning of the 1990 season Jim Leyland said that the Pirates were a legitimate contender and they would go as far as their pitching would take them. He was correct. It took them through an exhilarating season, during which they attracted more attendees than at any other time in their history, defeated the hated Mets at decisive times, earned Manager of the Year, Most Valuable Player and Cy Young awards, and seemed poised for a Cinderella finish before their good pitching was bested by the great pitching of Jose Rijo and the Nasties during the Championship Series.

In the 1991 season the same pattern prevailed. More than 2,000,000 fans attended that summer, setting an even higher record. Good pitching carried the Pirates into the Championship Series with the Atlanta Braves, but the young hard throwers from Georgia overpowered the Pirates totally ("splintered their bats," in the words of the Atlanta manager). Although Carl Barger and Larry Doughty have been replaced by Mark Sauer and Ted

Simmons as President and General Manager respectively, Jim Leyland's view of the game has not changed. The key to success remains, as he repeatedly states, pitching, pitching, pitching.

Being a major league city has always served to underline the importance of Pittsburgh in the national scheme of things. Major league cities need major league airports. Having concluded that the present international airport would not be adequate for Pittsburgh's needs in the 21st century, Commissioner Thomas J. Foerster led a coalition dedicated to the construction of a new, larger and more serviceable airport. Scheduled to open in 1992, the new airport is located within two miles of its predecessor, and, at a cost of $1,000,000,000, is being heralded as the most advanced of its genre. The architect chosen to design it was Tasso Katselas. (Ironically, Katselas, whose work is internationally known, was once under consideration to design a new international airport in Baghdad. He spent many months and much money on a special module only to see the project abandoned by the Iraqi government at the eleventh hour).

Because the new airport was being touted for its architectural excellences, *The New York Times* ran a major profile of it under the headline: PITTSBURGH AIRPORT OF FUTURE BEING BUILT. The article's author noted that the new airport would occupy 900 acres, have 76 gates, save the airlines $12,000,000 to $13,000,000 a year in fuel costs, create more than 81,000 jobs over the next twenty years and "mean as much to further development and diversification as it does to area aviation." It was also noted that an estimated cargo tonnage per year of 30,000,000 would be the highest for any inland city and that the architectural design would be the "most innovative" in the United States. Various public officials, including Commissioner Foerster, were named and deservedly credited for their enterprise and vigor. Businessmen salivated about the airport's potential for encouraging ancillary investment. There was only one man who was neither quoted nor mentioned: Tasso Katselas, the architect of the entire project.

While construction proceeded apace at the airport, there were other forces at work in the inner city (when does outer become inner?) as certain Pittsburgh landmarks were rubble-ized to make way for the new. Defenders of Pittsburgh's distinctive past openly opposed the demolition of St. Peter's Episcopal Church and the Syria Mosque, claiming that history alone should justify their preservation, quite apart from everything else. Developers had other ideas. In both cases the developers won, but the willingness of opponents to have the courage of a seemingly lost cause demonstrated conclusively that the new was not necessarily better just because it was new.

Ironically, it was the preservation of Pittsburgh's past in its streets, structures and neighborhoods (plus economic advantages) that drew filmmakers to Pittsburgh during the late eighties and early nineties. In fact, Pittsburgh now ranks third in the country (behind Hollywood and New York) as a hub of filmmaking. The Greater Pittsburgh Office of Promotion has even appointed a full-time coordinator to make sure that filmmakers continue to find Pittsburgh a hospitable place to work. Years earlier a maverick director named George Romero made a film called *Night of the Living Dead* in Pittsburgh with local actors and technicians. It not only became a cult classic for all those interested in ghoulish resurrections, but many say that it created the climate and the reservoir of technical and theatrical talent for what is happening now.

One of the first major films that used Pittsburgh as a setting and also a base of operations was the heavily funded *The Deer Hunter* in 1977. Robert De Niro was seen in a trucker's cap on and off location in his search for authenticity. Later it was not uncommon for Pittsburghers to see Colleen Dewhurst, Christopher Reeve, Jodie Foster, Anthony Hopkins, Nick Nolte, Jeremy Irons, Susan Sarandon, Bob Hoskins, Jack Nicholson and Danny DeVito either on the job or in various eateries in the city. But filmmakers and actors brought more than notoriety. They also brought dollars—more than $65,000,000 in the last two years alone.

One of Pittsburgh's assets to filmmakers is its "look." Jonathan Demme, the director of the much-Oscared *The Silence of the Lambs*, was openly effusive about on-camera Pittsburgh—its buildings, its hills, its streets. And the praise is, I think, deserved. There is a sense of history here in the geography and architecture that reflect the character of the past. This is something that cannot be created; it must be earned. It is totally absent, for example, in north Dallas, Texas, where the instant, pre-cast neighborhoods have a suddenness that accommodates but somehow does not welcome. The Pittsburgh-born actor Tom Atkins actually left California and returned to live in Pittsburgh because he missed the sheer reality of it. The playwright Jason Miller left Malibu for similar reasons to return to his birthplace, Scranton, Pennsylvania. When I asked him precisely why he did, he said, "Malibu has no alleys."

Pittsburgh's human assets are equally attractive to makers of movies (why do we persist in calling them movies—pictures that move—when they have long since become the talkies?). Technicians and local actors have found that the out-of-town filmmakers need them, and they have made their services readily available. W. Stephen Coleman, who acts under the name of Alex Coleman and who is the Chairman of the Theater Arts Department of the University of Pittsburgh, was given a role in *The Silence of the Lambs* because he bore a passing resemblance to Anthony Hopkins. Coleman, a seasoned actor and director, made the most of the coincidence.

Filmmaking companies are not the only non-indigenous institutions that have had an impact on Pittsburgh's economy. Miles Incorporated or Miles Inc. (formerly known as Bayer USA) is a German-owned company (there are more than 100 German-owned companies in Allegheny County, by the way) located on the high ground midway between Pittsburgh and the new international airport. Miles has additional offices in downtown Pittsburgh, but its array of sandbrown office buildings on the Parkway West is the eye-catcher. Officially Miles is known as a Chemical Health Care and Imaging Technologies Company, which means it makes everything from x-rays and aspirin to the chemicals needed for the production of compact discs. It also has a philosophy of involving its officials in community affairs. Konrad Weis, the former CEO and now honorary chairman of Miles Inc., is active with numerous cultural and charitable organizations, and Richard L. White, Corporate Executive Vice-President, is also President of the Board of Directors of Duquesne University, to name but two examples.

One of Miles' most innovative philanthropies (initiated when it was still Bayer USA) was the renovation of the first and only classical radio station in Pittsburgh, WQED-FM. Founded by a young visionary named Jack Sommers in 1973, the station was and remains devoted to undiluted hours of Beethoven, Bartok, Stravinsky, Bernstein, Bach, Mozart and others. (Its friendly competitor, WDUQ-FM, is the official station of Duquesne University. Although its format includes programs of classical music, it is the exclusive National Public Radio station in the city, which means that it carries "Morning Edition," "All Things Considered" together with "live" broadcasts from the National Press Club, Senate hearings and the like. It also has a virtual lock on the jazz audience in the city where jazz has a strong following. A program called the "Night Side" serves this burgeoning audience. It is hosted by Tony Mowod whose baritone voice and casual pacing are a perfect match for the music he broadcasts).

After Jack Sommers' sudden death in 1976, WQED-FM survived a few years of uncertainty before it came under the direction of Sommers' energetic and equally visionary widow, Ceci. Concise, decisive and a practical marketeer, Ceci Sommers consolidated both resources and staff and kept the station afloat and thriving. At the time she became acquainted with the aformentioned Konrad Weis. Little by little she attempted to interest Weis and the Bayer authorities in making a major contribution to WQED-FM to update and enlarge its studios and broadcasting facilities. The station, allowing for mountains and other interferences, has a hearing radius of 60 to 100 miles, and the modernization would, in Ceci Sommers' concept, confirm the presence of the station within that radius and beyond. Eventually Weis, in a spirit of enlightened self-interest, saw the wisdom of subvention and persuaded his associates to make a grant of half a million dollars to the station. In return WQED-FM would retain its call letters, but it would also be known as the Miles Broadcasting Center for the Arts. Thus, for $500,000 the name of Miles Inc. would, at every rising of the sun and the setting thereof and for all the hours in between and partially thereafter, reach listeners within a generous circumference of the city of Pittsburgh. As an example of visionary business philanthropy in which both the receiver and the giver benefit and mutually support one another's interests, this seems to be a classical model. Actually, Ceci Sommers created the motto for such a contributory spirit by announcing during her various on-the-air solicitations, "Give until it feels good." The cosmopolitan Konrad Weis, after making the half a million dollar grant, told her privately, "Ceci, Bayer USA feels so good today that it hurts."

Without doubt the best known and probably the most affluent of Pittsburgh's foreign-born industrial leaders is Dr. Anthony J. F. O'Reilly, Chairman, President and Chief Executive Officer of the H. J. Heinz Company. Many say he is one of the best corporate directors and managers in the world. The profits of the company under his leadership seem to bear this out (from a market capitalization of $908,000,000 in 1979 to $10,000,000,000 in 1991). But O'Reilly is no technocrat, a term he not only deplores but uses with derision when referring to others who actually are. Having become a kind of folk hero in Ireland because of his prowess as a rugby player (not only for Irish national teams but for the British and Irish "Lions" when they competed in South Africa, New Zealand and Australia), he subsequently earned a doctorate in agricultural marketing from the University of Bradford in Great Britain. O'Reilly then served as the managing director of the Irish Sugar Company and Erin Foods before joining Heinz.

In addition to professional competence, O'Reilly brought a continental flair to the position. When Heinz officials affirmed that they would not buy tuna from suppliers whose tuna fleets indiscriminately netted dolphin in the process, O'Reilly noted that the arguments among Heinz officials were "almost theological in tone." He not only can quote statistics and marketing strategies in the company of stockholders and staff, but can recite poetry from memory—and always when most appropriate. When he speaks of Irish matters, for example, he inserts verses by William Butler Yeats or Seamus Heaney to further illustrate his points. Once when he was stressing how situations and times could become permanently important if people only saw the universal in the particular, he quoted (again from memory) the following poem by Patrick Kavanagh called "Epic":

> I have lived in important places, time
> When great events were decided, who owned
> That half a rood of rock, a no-man's land
> Surrounded by our pitchfork-armed claims.
> I heard the Duffys shouting "Damn your soul!"
> And old McCabe stripped to the waist, seen
> Step the plot defying blue cast-steel—
> "Here is the march along these iron stones."
> That was the year of the Munich bother. Which
> Was more important? I inclined
> To lose my faith in Ballyrush and Gortin
> Till Homer's ghost came whispering to my mind.
> He said: I made the *Iliad* from such
> A local row. Gods make their own importance.

Nor is O'Reilly, like most of his fellow Irish, without levity. An after-dinner speaker and orator with a genuine sense of occasion, he is able to combine seriousness with humor in a way that somehow permits one to humanize the other. On one occasion I heard him suggest how the way something is said can influence and even dictate the answer desired. His illustration involved a Dominican and "the inevitable Jesuit." The Dominican wanted to know if it was permissible to pray and smoke. He consulted the Jesuit, and the Jesuit suggested that each of them consult in turn his respective superior. The Dominican returned and told the Jesuit that his superior, when asked if it was permissible "to smoke while I pray," refused him permission. The Jesuit said that his superior had indeed given him permission and even commended him for making the request, which was phrased as follows: "Is it permissible for me to pray while I'm smoking?"

Some would say that the presence of foreign-born chief executive officers in Pittsburgh is a sign of its growing cosmopolitanism. But such has been the fate of most of the major cities in the United States, if not the world. We see daily evidence of it in the medical profession, in academic life, in industry, in arts and even in some sports. In this sense the last decade of the twentieth century is radically different from the first decade or even the middle decades. But, although the cast has changed, the set has remained fundamentally the same. Spring happens in the parks named after Schenley and Frick as it always has. The numerous bridges in the county, though in need of repointing and retooling, continue to offer their graceful geometries to all who have eyes to see. The basic geography of the city, as Arthur C. Smith has documented in a superb, definitive book called *Pittsburgh Then and Now* (University of Pittsburgh Press, 1990), is one which Pittsburghers have befriended rather than distorted.

There is one feature in the city's changing profile, however, that is disturbing to many, and I include myself in this number. For some time now we Pittsburghers have been told that the city is changing from being production-oriented to being service-oriented. Statistics seem to bear this out. Today the ratio of service-related institutions to manufacturers of primary metals is approximately six to one. The fact that this is now happening is

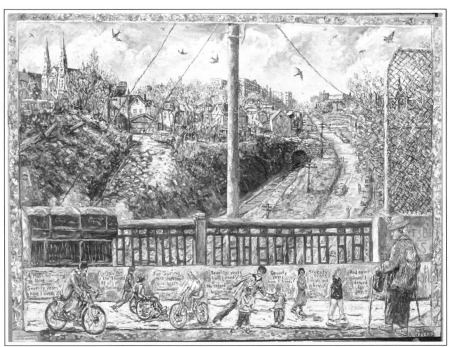

Spring Bridge, 1983.

regarded by some as a matter of historical inevitability, as if blind acceptance is the only conceivable response to such a radical change in our civic character. But what does such a change presage for us and quite possibly, if the trend is more than local, for the United States as a whole? It implies, to be blunt about it, that we should accustom ourselves to becoming, not creators or producers, but middlemen, handlers, go-betweens, deliverers. Compute it, data-base it, raise it to the umpteenth power, translate it into sociologese or public-relationese, and the conclusion is the same. What it comes down to is that service-oriented cities serve the real producers; they move, sell, advertise or distribute the goods produced by others.

Statistics indicate that service-related institutions do provide employment for many of the men and women rendered jobless by this "historic change." Given this scenario, employment is always preferable to destitution or mandatory re-location—at least the option of employment. Nor do I mean to slight those speciality-steel companies like Metaltech and World Class Processing Inc. that have been created by enlightened owners, managers and workers and meet a definite need in the steel industry. It has been estimated that 30% to 35% of the work force in the city is involved in such speciality production, and that is all to the good. But, philosophically speaking, what is lost when a city changes from being a producer of steel from basic ores and fuels to being a machino-facturer or servicer?

One thing that is lost, of course, is pride in creation. The bridgers of Ambridge took longstanding pride in saying once that every bridge in the United States was made with steel produced in Ambridge, Pennsylvania, by the American Bridge Company. And Governor Mario Cuomo told a Pittsburgh audience in the fall of 1988 that the combined output of Aliquippa, Carnegie and Homestead in their heydays outproduced the world. If this is true, and if Winston Churchill was correct in claiming that steel was the essential component without which World War II could not have been waged and eventually won, then it could be concluded that the war was won right here in southwest Pennsylvania.

The essential difference between those who produce and those who distribute is the difference between the creator and the agent. If Pittsburgh (and possibly the entire country) is facing the loss or the diminution of its productive capacities, what effect will this have on people—on their working habits and, more importantly, their self-esteem?

I have already mentioned that one sure loss is pride in creation. This was brought home to me several years ago when a friend told me that he had an office opposite the rising superstructure of the now completed

Liberty Center. The fact that every girder was stamped MADE IN KOREA left him wincing every time he looked out of his window. I'm sure this story has echoes in many other phases of Pittsburgh life. Why? The answer may be that every city creates its true character not by marketing the goods of others but by placing its stamp on those things that only it can create. In Ireland, for example, Waterford crystal is inseparable from the city of Waterford itself, and the people of that city (and of the entire country, for that matter) take a deep national pride in Waterford products. For the Swiss it is clocks, watches and Bally shoes. For the Germans, the Mercedes-Benz. For the French, the internationally famous trademarks of chic, scents and cuisine. For the Italians, the creations of Gucci and the uniqueness of the Alfa Romeo and the Testarosa.

Fortunately, there remain in Pittsburgh a number of industries that continue to be productive and to serve needs at home and abroad. The aforementioned H.J. Heinz Company, which is presently planning a new $100,000,000 plant on the North Side, is the most obvious example. No matter where in the world they travel, many Pittsburghers insist on having Heinz ketchup—a true compliment to the product and its producers as well as living proof of the fungibility of local pride. Another Pittsburgh producer is the Three Rivers Aluminum Company (TRACO). Five years ago I wrote that TRACO was awarded the commission to replace the bronze windows in the crown of the Statue of Liberty. Since then the same company was contracted to replace all the windows in the Empire State Building. In these two instances alone I think that any Pittsburgher would take a certain conscious or subconscious pride in knowing that Pittsburgh-based companies were producing things that, in national or international circumstances, were judged as the best of their kind and were chosen as such for use. It permits people to say that such-and-such was made *in* Pittsburgh instead of saying that such-and-such was distributed *through* Pittsburgh. If you don't think that the verbs make a difference, just say each of those clauses aloud and listen to the one with the deeper ring.

I suppose the point I am trying to make is that producers and creators, not middle-men or distributors, authenticate and nail-down a culture. When a city loses its productive and creative character, it loses something of its soul. It begins to shrink, spiritually. It cannot take refuge in the fact that "change is inevitable and ineluctable" and act as if the character of the city will remain the same. Change is not always progress. Moreoever, blind acceptance of mere change characterizes men who are no longer actors but reactors. In the name of realism such reactors accept and adjust to whatever history dishes up to them. By such a standard "reactors" will accept defeat as readily as victory, regression as well as advancement, the best as well as the worst.

Paradoxically at the present moment there are a number of creative artists in the city who are contributing to its creative core (as the production of steel contributed to its productive core in past years) and making Pittsburgh a name to conjure with in literature, art, theatrical productions and jazz. Even though their work more often than not transcends city

Millworker, 1975. Panel for light pole produced in cooperation with the Steel Industry Heritage Corporation and the Homestead Economic Recovery Corporation, 1996.

boundaries, it is still the city that is the beneficiary of their significance and renown. In a city known once for its basic industries, these artists are showing that poetry, fiction, drama, art, dance and music have a staying power more durable than steel itself.

As one who was born in Pittsburgh, I have the indigenous allegiance of the native. But quite apart from that I have discovered over the years that I am never totally happy (an awkward word in this context, but I can't think of an alternative) when I am away from Pittsburgh for a protracted period of time. I not only miss friends, my work, my house and the usual familiarities, but I also miss the geography and the architectural visuals. From the top of Mt. Washington at night I have often looked far up the Allegheny River—bridge by lighted bridge—with the awe a German might have if he looked up the Rhine from a similar angle. I have felt completely at home beside the man-scaled structures of the South Side. I have walked through the marble and mahogany and bronze perfection of the Union Trust Building as if I were strolling through the Vatican or the Louvre. I have enjoyed the perpetual youth of Kennywood Park. I have seen the skyline signature of Pittsburgh's downtown from north, east, south and west and know what it takes for a city to be defined as a twentieth century metropolis. I have seen and felt the seasons come and stay and go in all their different beauty and unpredictability. In brief, I live in a city where I am never bored, and that is as good a synonym for love that I know.

1998

I begin this section by paraphrasing what I wrote six years ago.

Ask me where I was born, and I will say the place exists no more except within me—literally inside of me. Where else is history but there in each of us? Tens of thousands of Pittsburghs (each dawn reveals a similarly different city) have come into existence since I arrived on the scene. And many thousands will follow. No city (or no country, for that matter) stays the same. Granted, a city may remain within certain geographical boundaries, but within those boundaries there is continual destruction, construction and reconstruction. Some of the destruction may be due to entropy, but most will be the result of the desire within us to get rid of the no longer functional or beautiful or serviceable and replace it with something else—hopefully but certainly not always something better.

In this sense Pittsburgh does not differ from other American cities. But if you've lived in Pittsburgh all your life, as I have, and if changes continue to happen all around you, you often are overwhelmed, not by the reality but by the unreality of it all. As a teenager when I went downtown I could see a multiplicity of movie houses: the Alvin, the Barry, the Warner, the Loew's Penn (now Heinz Hall), the Stanley (now the Benedum), the Newsreel on Fourth Avenue where only newsreels were featured, and the Art Cinema where films like the birth of a baby were shown as if childbirth were the most risque thing imaginable in those Jansenistic days. The Stanley was my favorite. In its prime I could go there and see all the big bands and their bandleaders perform on its stage—Benny Goodman, Tommy and Jimmy Dorsey, Woody Herman, Duke Ellington, Count Basie, Lionel Hampton, Artie Shaw, Fats Waller, Harry James, Vaughn Monroe, Gene Krupa and Glenn Miller, to name only the most prominent.

And then there were the indispensable and absolutely reliable department stores—not only Kaufmann's and Gimbels (now gone) and Joseph Horne's (now gone) but Frank & Seder's, Boggs & Buhl's and Rosenbaum's. Yet even as I write these names and think of the names of other stores, moviehouses, downtown shops of long standing like Volkwein's (now off the Parkway West) and restaurants like Dutch Henry's where the corned beef sandwiches were inimitable and where photographs of President Roosevelt or of Billy Conn and Fritzie Zivic (both in fighters' togs) stared at you from their sacred positions above the cash register, I cannot help but wonder if all these places ever existed.

Of course, there remain permanent reminders of Pittsburgh's past

Allegheny County Jail, 1995.

that have not to date disappeared. The most prominent examples are the county jail and courthouse. Designed by Henry Hobbs Richardson and completed in 1887 (Richardson did not live to see the completion of his last and, in his opinion, his most accomplished architectural commission), the complex of jail and courthouse gives a sense of medieval *gravitas* to the downtown area. The courthouse is still in daily use, but the jail has been succeeded by a new jail of apartment-like proportions between Second Avenue and the Parkway bordering the Monongahela River. Richardson's jail, which is made entirely of granite, has the look of a European fortress, and even the casual observer cannot help but note the size of the granite blocks and then wonder how the construction engineers lifted and levered them into position. There is talk of converting the jail into a museum. It would make an excellent one, particularly if it could preserve for posterity a history of Pittsburgh's architecture, including the incomparable river architecture of its bridges. But more about bridges later. In the meanwhile, Richardson's granite buildings are there to remind us that some things can and do defy change, if only for a time.

On second thought, why should this strike me as such a mystery? Shouldn't I realize that life is synonymous with change and that city life is certainly not exempt? But just as something in all of us yearns to be what we were (with some exceptions, of course), there is also something within us that wants the familiar landscapes of memory to remain forever as we first knew them. When they don't (and they invariably don't), we feel slightly disoriented and even more than slightly alienated.

One of Pittsburgh's most salient aspects of change is its growing cosmopolitanism from mid-century to the present. Foreign nationals were not as plentiful in the city in the fifties. Now they are so evident that their presence has become commonplace, not only among students but in the professional classes as well. One hears numerous foreign languages spoken openly where formerly they were spoken only within residences. Restaurants now cater to a myriad of tastes, and each cuisine has its devoted clientele: Northern Italian, Spanish, Middle Eastern, German, Indian, Chinese, Irish, Cambodian, Vietnamese, Japanese, Jewish, Peruvian, Taiwanese, Calabrian and French.

The make-up of student bodies has changed. A university like Duquesne used to draw the decisive majority of its students from the tri-state area. Now it openly and proudly announces that all fifty states are represented in its student body as well as students from eighty-one foreign countries. I have no doubt that other universities and colleges in the area would be able to come up with similar statistics. This has caused many educators in all these institutions to wonder if the change in the student population will presage a change in the very character of higher learning in the city and how it is "marketed" to draw prospective students here. Proponents of diversification argue that such cosmopolitanism is the only way universities and colleges can survive in the current climate. Those with reservations say that universities run the risk of adulterating their basic disciplines by creating programs that cater only to the vocational interests of students in order to attract them, regardless of their states or countries of origin. They say that Pittsburgh's collegiate institutions are becoming more and more corporately structured so as to draw and keep undergraduates and graduate students who in effect are often there not to engage in the dispassionate quest for truth but to earn the degree that will be their ticket to job security and professional advancement. Too often in such circumstances the students are seen as customers while the faculty tend to be regarded simply as employees in the service of the corporate goals of their respective institutions.

In this respect it is appropriate to recount an incident that occurred during Dwight Eisenhower's first meeting with the faculty at Columbia University shortly after he was installed as its President. He began the meeting by addressing the gathered professors as "Employees of Columbia University . . . ." One professor then rose and said, "President Eisenhower, we are not employees of Columbia University. We are Columbia University." One cannot help but wonder if such a spirit is on the wane in universities generally as well as locally, and, if so, what effect this will have on higher learning in the country as a whole. In the January 4, 1998 edition of *The New York Times* James Shapiro warned of the consequences of this radical change in what a university should be: "The danger today is that the administrations that now set policy at most universities are increasingly tempted to act as if they are running a business—letting profit motives drive educational policy. In such a climate, revenue-generating programs and inexpensive part-time professors are winning out over a committed faculty, good libraries and small classes. American universities have achieved their international prominence precisely because they have, until now, recognized the value of free inquiry, open expression and discovery that is driven not by financial gain but by broader social ends. The crisis on today's campus is not, as the news media would have it, about the culture wars but about the almost impossible choices that will have to be made if universities are to lead, not merely imitate, a rapidly changing society."

Further accenting Pittsburgh's cosmopolitanism are the number of industries in the city and county that are foreign-owned. Currently there are more than 150 industries that so qualify. Of these, 62 are German-owned, 27 British, 14 Canadian, 12 Japanese and sundry others whose owners are Australian, Austrian, Belgian, Brazilian, Czechoslovakian, Danish, Finnish, French, Indian, Israeli, Italian, Korean, Dutch, Norwegian, Swedish and Swiss. These firms deal in everything from mining machinery and metal products to glass containers, cements, locks, chemicals, alloys, optical equipment, wood veneer, stainless steel, cookies, printing presses, plastics, pharmaceuticals, television sets, windows, window shades, ceramics and office furniture. Any Pittsburghers who persist in believing that they are still provincial and living an insular existence need only look around to be disabused of this illusion.

In December of 1992 Pittsburgh, like too many other cities in the country, became a one-newspaper city. The *Pittsburgh Press* ceased to exist, and the *Pittsburgh Post-Gazette* went on alone—or at least historically alone since the *Tribune-Review*, based in Greensburg, tried to capture its share of the Pittsburgh market by publishing a Pittsburgh edition of the paper. At last count the *Review*'s circulation was notably in arrears of that of the *Post-Gazette*. The P-G's daily circulation is approximately 243,000 while its Sunday circulation is slightly over 424,000. In contrast the Greensburg-based paper has a daily circulation of 84,000 while its Sunday circulation is under 145,000. What does this prove? It shows, I believe, that readers keep a habitual loyalty to what they have gotten used to over the years and do not automatically accept replacements. And it also tends to show that Pittsburghers, though conservative in the slow-to-change-without thinking-something-through sense, are not as conservative (some say reactionary) as the spirit of the *Tribune-Review*'s editorials and the philosophy of the owner and publisher, Richard Scaife, are known to be.

But circulation and political orientation notwithstanding, the question to be asked (and hopefully answered) is whether Pittsburgh is better off without having two newspapers of longstanding influence and comparable stature. It should also be kept in mind that the *Press* was an afternoon and not a morning newspaper. (It is possible that the *Tribune-Review*'s smaller circulation in Pittsburgh at the moment is because of the fact that it is competing with the *Post-Gazette* in a market that the latter has had to itself for decades). The absence of an afternoon daily left a real void, despite all that has been and will continue to be said about television as a replacement for print journalism and how most people (regrettably, I think) get most if not all of their news from television. This means that breaking news stories must wait for the morning editions of the day following the event in question to be reported in their entirety, particularly since the newspaper "extra" is a thing of the past. At no time was this more painfully evident than when USAirways Flight 407 crashed in Hopewell Township while coming in for a landing at Pittsburgh International Airport. People woke up the next morning and scoured the *Post-Gazette* for the names of those on the plane. The officials at USAirways had not by then released the manifest, but they did release the names at mid-day. An afternoon newspaper would have been able to print the names of the doomed passengers and spared many readers the agony of hours of suspense.

Those who think that Pittsburgh is better off with only one *bona fide* Pittsburgh newspaper should consider the example of New York. Is New York a better city, journalistically speaking, since the *Herald Tribune* closed its doors and left the field to the *Times* and the tabloids? Also, those who say that major American cities are not really able to support two or more metropolitan dailies should be reminded that the city of Beirut, Lebanon, during the darkest days of its internal strife while it was encircled by an invading army and under seige still managed to publish 35 newspapers daily.

Everyone who knows Pittsburgh will admit that it is in essence a city

Detail of *Steelworker* Mural, Forbes Avenue, Oakland, 1990.

of and for workers. Whether motivated by the Protestant ethic (an honorable code of behavior despite the belittlement that has recently been visited upon it) or the immigrants' urgency to survive or the desire of the more recent generations to "make it" or the simple and sacred desire of a man or woman to do a "good job," the reliance upon work as a dominant force in social life is a given. It was not by accident, for example, that the tradition of trade unionism was nurtured here. Nor was it by accident that many of those who became prosperous here more often than not (in contrast to the affluent of more recent vintage) returned a portion of their wealth to the city where they earned it. The names of Carnegie and Mellon come to mind in this regard, particularly the name of Paul Mellon whose munificence not only to the city but in Washington and throughout the United States is almost beyond comparison in the annals of American philanthropy.

The tradition of work might explain public resistance to suggestions that riverboat gambling be introduced here on the pretext that it would "provide jobs" for Pittsburghers. The sponsors of this idea used the more euphemistic word "gaming" to make the suggestion more palatable to the public. In addition, one advocate strove to purify the idea further by stating that there was not a word against gambling in the *Bible*. He saw it as wholesome adult entertainment for those who could afford it. A majority of Pittsburghers saw through this travesty immediately as would anyone who would take it upon himself to read Dostoyevsky's *The Gambler* or even casually consider the attendant vices that gambling invariably brings with it, of which the greed for quick and easy money is the least offensive. With or without Dostoyevsky the public rejected the idea out of hand.

The current idea of replacing Three Rivers Stadium with two others—one for baseball, one for football—on the North Side has generated both support and skepticism. Supporters argue that football and baseball can survive on a nationally competitive level only if each sport has its own venue. The playing surface (grass instead of artificial turf) is not the key problem, nor is it a question of parking and accessibility. Supporters realize that new venues would contain lucrative corporate box seats and many other assets, generating revenues that the owners of the Pirates and Steelers believe would permit them to meet the rising costs associated with the maintenance of their franchises. The skeptics, who are largely from the tax-paying public, question whether taxes should be used for what is after all in their eyes a pair of businesses—albeit businesses that are an integral part of civic pride. The skeptics are not wildly but only moderately opposed, and this is partly because even the most recalcitrant among them realize at heart that this really may be "a done deal." In favor of the change are the Pirate and Steelers owners, Mayor Thomas Murphy, Governor Thomas Ridge, a majority of county commissioners and various business leaders. Opposed are the aforementioned skeptics and numerous conservatives to whom the whole idea smells of porkbarreling. And there the matter stands at this writing.

All things want to fly, Union Trust Building, 1988.

Regardless of how the stadium matter is resolved, it brings home to me how many proposals for civic renewal of one type or another deal with entertainment—gambling as entertainment, sports as entertainment and so on. Most Americans realize that the need to make everything entertaining from television news to media advertising to academic learning to religious belief is part of the national mood. But any mature person knows

A Book of Hours, 3 p.m. Ritual, 1987. Poem by Jane McCreery.

that this is at odds with the nature of life itself, which finds its fulfillment by surviving in the face of struggle and not in the midst of diversions and hurrahs. People who work know this instinctively, and Pittsburgh is a city, as I have suggested, where the work ethic predominates. Newcomers who have attempted to re-make the city in a different image have not had much success over the years. Anything that does not have the smell or promise of sweat about it probably will not survive here, and those who think otherwise are eventually driven to the periphery by the centrifugal force of civic life itself.

Of course, we have other problems that cannot go unmentioned. Though Pittsburgh's crime rate is decreasing along with the national average, there are still too many instances of domestic or gang quarrels settled by gunfire. And drive-by shootings happen from time to time (usually just long enough to be branded "senseless" as if "sensible" drive-by shootings would be more acceptable). And there are many neighborhoods in Pittsburgh that would benefit from revitalization the sooner the better. And the safety of city streets for pedestrians is not yet total.

As if in counterpoint to these and other ongoing problems, the city was the scene of a number of happenings, both bad and good, that brought it to the attention of the country as a whole. There was the already mentioned crash of USAirways Flight 407 in Hopewell Township for reasons that are still somewhat a mystery. Imagining a jet suddenly diving nose first into the ground from just a few thousand feet in the air is enough to put a dagger through anyone's heart. For all of us who remember this event when it happened, that image and that feeling persist and probably will for the rest of our lives.

A similar horrific memory was forged when a tornado devastated a street in Mt. Washington on June 2, 1998 and then went on to havoc some contiguous areas in the southwestern section of the state. Three deaths were reported (none in the city), but many people were immediately disabused of the idea that urban and mountainous areas were tornado-immune. I drove by Virginia Avenue in Mt. Washington a day after the storm. Most of the residents had piled downed branches and limbs for pick-up at the curbs, but the numerous destroyed trees that had not been cut into sections for removal looked as if some Gulliver had stomped through the neighborhood and ripped them from the roots like so many celery stalks. And then, of course, there was the destruction done to houses and automobiles, i.e., shredded rooftops, brick chimneys wind-sledged to rubble, rooms full of imploding window glass waiting to be broomed away, the dented and gashed hoods of parked cars. KDKA-TV, which preempted its regular programs to keep its announcers on the air continuously, was credited with saving the lives of many by peremptorily telling those in the tornado's predicted path to take cover in their basements immediately.

Not all the news that gained national notice for Pittsburgh had to do with disasters. Martha Rial, a staff photographer for the *Pittsburgh Post-Gazette*, took photographs of the plight of refugees in Rawanda while she was visiting her sister there. The photos were significant enough to earn her a Pulitzer Prize.

The city's writers continue to demonstrate to all who notice that Pittsburgh is literally a city for writers. Novelists, biographers, essayists, fictioneers, playwrights and, above all, poets are creating names for themselves that transcend their local addresses. Perhaps in recognition of their achievements the *Pittsburgh Post-Gazette* initiated a policy several years ago of printing a poem on its *op. ed.* page every Saturday morning, not as a filler but as a prominent and framed feature. Many readers make a special point of making sure they purchase and read these Saturday poems without fail. And the poets benefit as well. Jim Daniels, an award-winning poet who teaches at Carnegie Mellon University, told me that more people had read his *op. ed.* poem than had read all of his books combined.

In the field of sports, the Pittsburgh Steelers under Bill Cowher's style of coaching and the steady managerial hand of Dan Rooney made a habit of winning division titles but have still been denied the crown of the Super Bowl. Few doubt that these winning ways will not continue. But the fate of the Pittsburgh Pirates was and remains an ongoing saga. Purchased by youthful Kevin McClatchy after other bidders were rejected, the new Pirate management faced and still faces the formidable challenge of convincing a skeptical public that a small-market team can be competitive. McClatchy himself, whose cousin is the editor of *The Yale Review* and whose maternal grandfather is George F. Kennan, the seminal architect of and most important influence upon our country's foreign policy from the end of World War II to the present, is not an absentee owner. He calls himself a "younser," took up residence in Pittsburgh and is invariably seen in the stands behind home plate in game after game. As if in response to some visceral allegiance not only to the city but to the spirit of baseball itself, the Pirates became the talk of the league in the 1997 season. They played commendable baseball with a combination of rookies and journeymen and stayed in spirited contention with Houston for the division title until the very last days of the season. In short, they made the summer of 1997 a summer to remember and caused many to re-think the idea that only well-heeled franchises in cities like New York, Chicago, Los Angeles and San Francisco could dream of championships. All that Pittsburghers needed to be reminded of was the World Series of 1960 when the "dismissable" Pirates defeated the "unbeatable" Yankees in seven games to show that David's defeat of Goliath was not a fluke and could happen again. In that spirit they supported the team, and they continue to do so.

Numerous theories have been advanced about what draws people together. Disasters like tornados certainly do. Pride in sports franchises has the same unifying dynamism. But why pursue each disquisitions? What is integral is that, despite natural upheavals or citizen achievements in sports or academics or the professions, there are overarching considerations that unify a population no matter how contentious the controversies may be that divide them or how persistent the phenomena that distract them. The common denominator of mortality itself is enough to make us realize that we share what all mortals share, in Pittsburgh or anywhere. We hope for the continued well-being of our children and those we love. We fear suf-

Westinghouse Bridge—Crossing, 1988.

fering, violence and death. We admire the beautiful, the truthful and the heroic. And we eventually come to recognize and, if gifted by faith, profess our belief in a power or powers greater than ourselves. These bridge all of our temporary differences.

Pittsburgh is fortunate to have the very symbols of our unity as people as part of its civic architecture—an omnipresent part. These are its bridges. There are some 800 bridges in the city proper and more than 2100 in Allegheny County. No other county in the country rivals this number, and many of these bridges were designed by some of the most distinguished architects of the time—Roebling, Lindenthal and others.

Most of us look at bridges as feats of engineering and nothing more. But they are as much agents of unity as poetry is. Both poetry and bridges spring from the imagination of their creators. They have an inherent grace and power that can stop us in our tracks. Imaginatively speaking, a bridge is a road through and in space. It spans distance by the most direct means possible, stitching together permanently separated shores by the medium of itself. Like poetry it binds, uniting, uniting, uniting.

Railroad Bridge, East Liberty, 1969.

The American poet Hart Crane saw a bridge as a "communication . . . a symbol of consciousness spanning time and space." He could easily have been speaking of poetry. In this sense we Pittsburghers are fortunate to be reminded daily how bridges return us to our common roots just as poetry does. Bridges are examples of material designed by man to defy impossibility as gracefully and strongly as possible. If we regard our treasury of bridges not only as an architectural trove but as a poetic one, we can appreciate the poetry of what is bountifully all around us and which is ours for the acknowledging. In the process we just might discover the deeper and more universal self that lives, like history, within each of us.

Everytime I see or cross a bridge I find myself ready to be more pleasant. I have no explanation for this. It usually happens to me by surprise, by reflex. Regardless, I'm always grateful for whatever puts me in a better mood whether the cause is a bridge or an incident. One incident that stands out in my recollection occurred at the Pittsburgh International Airport. I was waiting in the middle of a concourse. People were hurrying by on either side of me, and I must have been thinking of something that was making me frown. Suddenly a man sauntered up to me, stopped and said, "Smile, you're in Pittsburgh." My frown vanished instantly, and I smiled. Lately, I've surprised friend and stranger alike by saying, "Smile, you're in Pittsburgh," and the result is always a smile. Try it yourselves, and you'll see that the result will be the same. Whether this will become a replacement for our usual forms of greeting is unpredictable, but I for one give it my vote. Regardless, it's as good a note as any on which to bring this book to a close.

2003

As I have written in the three previous edition of this book, Pittsburgh is a work in progress. Of course, this is true of all cities as it is of life itself. But the resultant changes often leave us with a sense of unreality as the new begins to obscure what we remember. Then, as the new proceeds to establish its own "temporary" sense of permanence, we wonder if the old ever really existed in the first place. The result is that we live not only in the city that we see but also in the city of memory that pre-dates the present and underscores it with images that exist nowhere but within us. Perhaps this is why writers like T. S. Eliot in "The Wasteland" and Ernest Hemingway in his fiction and his non-fiction implied or frankly stated that only the names of cities (and countries) existed. The rest they saw as ephemera.

Having lived in Pittsburgh all my life, I have come to accept the verdicts of Eliot and Hemingway. True, the names of cities do not change. But everything else about them seems to be changing all the time. This is something that goes beyond urban sprawl and city planning and the like. It's more than sociology, more than architecture, more than renewal and much more than image. No matter what Pittsburgh conjures as a name, it has associations that have attached themselves to it over many years. I will not enumerate them, but they date from the years before the Revolutionary War to the present. One thing that seems to me to be consistently true about Pittsburgh is that it does not have a prototypical image that it feels it must live up to or not be itself. Compare it to New York, for example. New York is in perpetual pursuit of itself, and that self is believed to be what it presumes it is—the city of Broadway, Wall Street, the Village, Central Park and the rest. In short, the Big Apple. In contrast Pittsburgh in my view is not in competition with itself. It just goes on being what it turns out to be at its own speed and in its own way.

I have not mentioned T. S. Eliot and Ernest Hemingway by accident. I have cited them because their words as writers expressed a vision of the ultimate realities of cities (their names) that might strike most of us as being apocalyptic, even foreboding. But as artists that's what they sensed, and I for one take what they say to heart. Troy and Carthage are no more, but as names they still exist. No matter what is in Pittsburgh's future, it will always be known by its name.

The visions of writers and artists are crucial to the life of any city, and woe unto the city that derides or banishes or otherwise stultifies them. If intellectual conformity is the dominant "ism" of our time, it is the arts that stand for intellectual and spiritual individuality and independence. They exist to remind us of who we really are. They mirror us to ourselves whether we like what we see or not, and they tell us what we truly know but which we sometimes forget.

It is to Pittsburgh's credit that it is home to numerous writers, poets, artists, sculptors, actors, dancers and musicians. It is also to its credit that a strong alliance exists between artistic non-profit organizations and private and corporate foundations that are based here. Without such an alliance many non-profit groups would be unable to function. Why? Because one of the basic truths common to all not-for-profit organizations is that they survive through the largesse and generosity of those who believe in them and, above all, that they learn to lose money as slowly and wisely as possible. In a capitalistic democracy this does not bulk large in the day-to-day calculations of bottom-liners, but a supported and thriving life of the arts in any city is essential to its belief in itself, its culture, its potentiality. It is something that cannot be measured with the usual barometers of profit and loss. Art marches to a different drummer.

It seems that both foundations and individuals in Pittsburgh recognize the importance of the arts by the simple fact that they support them through contributions and attendance. The major contributions come from the private and corporate foundations already mentioned, and the smaller contributions from individuals, who also are the ticket-buyers who constitute the audience.

A few years ago the Pittsburgh Cultural Trust published an executive summary entitled *Economic and Social Impact of the Not-for-Profit-Arts Community in Allegheny Country and the City of Pittsburgh.* The conclusions presented in this summary were the result of a survey of sixty-three performing and visual arts organizations in the area, and it is enlightening to know their names since they reveal the sheer diversity of artistic activity here: The Acting Company, Afro-American Music Institute, the Andy Warhol Museum, Associated Artists of Pittsburgh, Bach Choir of Pittsburgh, Calliope, Carnegie Mellon University Drama Department, Carnegie Museum of Art, Chartiers Valley Arts Council, Chatham Baroque,

The Children's Festival Chorus, Children of Love Theatre, City Theatre, Community Media, The Frick Art and Historical Center, Gargaro Productions, Gateway to the Arts, I Dream a World, International Poetry Forum, Jazz at the Hill House, Jazz Workshop, Kingsley Association, Kuntu Repertory Theatre at the University of Pittsburgh, Lesbian and Gay Film Festival of Pittsburgh, Manchester Craftsmen's Guild, Mary Miller Dance Company, Mattress Factory, McKeesport Symphony Orchestra, Mendelssohn Choir of Pittsburgh, Monroeville Arts Council, Pittsburgh Ballet Theatre, Pittsburgh Camarata, Pittsburgh Center for the Arts, Pittsburgh Chamber Music Society, Pittsburgh CLO, the Pittsburgh Cultural Trust, Pittsburgh Dance Alloy, Pittsburgh Dance Council, Pittsburgh Filmmakers, Pittsburgh International Children's Theater, Pittsburgh International Folk Theatre, The Pittsburgh New Music Ensemble, Pittsburgh Opera, Pittsburgh Opera Theater, Pittsburgh Public Theater, Pittsburgh Symphony Orchestra, Physical Theatre Project, Quantum Theatre, The Renaissance & Baroque Society of Pittsburgh, Renaissance City Wind Music Society, River City Brass Band, Saltworks Theatre Company, Silver Eye Center for Photography, Society for Contemporary Crafts, South Arts, St. Mary Law-

Mellon Square, 1983.

renceville Arts, Sweetwater Center for the Arts, Three Rivers Arts Festival, Three Rivers Lecture Series, Three Rivers Young Peoples Orchestras, the Upstairs Theater and the Y Music Society.

The summary goes on to state that the aforementioned arts organizations, inclusive of their audiences and their employees, generate an economic benefit to Allegheny County in the amount of $368,000,000 per annum. In addition, these organizations have an annual business impact on Pittsburgh alone in the range of $251,000,000. Add to this approximately $1,100,000 in hotel revenues averaged out on a yearly basis. The totals of these figures are not negligible numbers, and those who are persuaded by figures alone should take them quite seriously, as the Pittsburgh Cultural Trust surely intended by publishing the summary.

Although these fiduciary benefits are certainly persuasive to those who measure worth exclusively in terms of money, do they really focus on the human importance of the arts to Pittsburgh or to any city in the world for that matter? If the arts did not bring a dime to the city's coffers, would they still be regarded as beneficial and even indispensable to civic life? If history is to be believed, the answer is an absolute yes. Not that the arts or artists start out with the idea of making a profit for themselves and others. Artistic creation derives from much deeper impulses. Indeed art often manages to come into existence where artistic creation is least expected. But, once created, art generates an unstoppable dynamism. One of the best explanations of the inevitability of art's staying power and why its originality can never be gainsaid has been proclaimed explicitly by E. M. Forster: "The work of art is the only material object in the universe which may possess internal harmony. All the others have been pressed into shape from outside, and when the mould is removed they collapse. The work of art stands up by itself, and nothing else does. It achieves something which has always been promised by society, but always delusively."

Without protracting a defense of the arts further than necessary in this consideration, I suspect that the main reason for art's ineluctable dynamism is that art is to society what the soul is to the body. Man, unlike other animals, cannot live by bread alone. The arts quite literally animate us as vitally as breath does. They will assuredly survive and endure with or without support because they fulfill man's need to experience the beautiful. Just as the mind fulfills itself through the natural act of learning (whether this learning is put to practical use or not), so does the soul breathe in the necessary oxygen of beauty through dance, music, painting, literature, sculpture and theater.

If these statements are justifiable, it simply stands to reason that any society should support the arts as something that is in its own interest to do.

This does not mean that the artists become the stewards of their sponsors. Nor does it mean that the relation between artists and society will always be amicable. In recent American history there was a political reaction to the whole idea of the arts being supported by public money. An institution as unique and helpful as the National Endowment for the Arts was attacked as having been the conduit for the support of projects that offended public sensibilities. Some wanted the Endowment to be scrapped entirely. Others defended its record and purpose. The result was that the Endowment survived but with a trimmed budget and with the ongoing onus of being in the gunsights of those who were just waiting to be further offended. In such an atmosphere the NEA was less able to support cultural centers and facilities than it had done previously, and this in turn caused many of these centers and facilities throughout the country to go out of existence.

Pittsburgh's history vis-à-vis the arts during this era (and so far it is ongoing) is in some ways exemplary. The alliance of Pittsburgh philanthropy and the arts asserted itself, and many organizations and individuals in the private sector rallied to fill the void created by the shrinking and intimidation of the National Endowment for the Arts. Indeed they did so even though they openly admitted that this support could not be sustained indefinitely without government assistance. The assistance of city and county government was of even more crucial help at this time and has continued since. In one year before the turn of the century, for example, city government funded 31 not-for-profit organizations for a total of $221,361, and the Allegheny Regional Asset District (ARAD), which derives its resources from sales taxes in the county, distributed grants to 88 not-for-profits during the same period for a total of $64,775,000, of which $59,338,500 went to arts organizations. Some have said that Pittsburgh's philanthropy in this era could be considered a national model, and they may have a point. After all, enlightened cultures from the Age of Pericles to the Florence of the Medicis have realized that support for the arts, regardless of controversy or friction, enhances society by enriching the lives of its citizenry.

At this point I would like to cite the example of one cultural institution in Pittsburgh that I know rather intimately, having founded it and been its director since 1966—the International Poetry Forum. The purpose of the Forum is to present programs of poetry (by the poets themselves or by actors) for the benefit and enjoyment of the paying public. For thirty-six years the Forum has hosted approximately 800 poets and performers, and its programs have been attended by thousands over that period.

What effect has an institution like the International Poetry Forum had on the cultural and social life of Pittsburgh? Has it been positive or negative? How did it take root in the city in the first place? For anyone wishing to evaluate the value of the Forum as a civic institution, these are important questions, and they require candid answers. The International Poetry Forum from its inception drew audiences from what can only be described as a population-in-waiting. People left their homes on pleasant or rainy nights and paid to hear poetry spoken from the stage directly to them. That this could happen in Pittsburgh surprised many people, but these are the same people who forget that poetry speaks to anyone and everyone regardless of location or reputation. This certainly proved to the case in Pittsburgh where audiences came regularly to hear poets like Richard Wilbur, Robert Lowell, Archibald MacLeish, Yevgeny Yevtushenko, Linda Pastan, Mary Oliver, Billy Collins, Maxine Kumin, John Berryman, Lawrence Durrell, Thomas Kinsella, Seamus Heaney, Evan Boland, Tomas Transtromer, Anthony Hecht, John Ciardi, Miller Williams, Mona Van Duyn and countless others. They came with equal fervor to hear poets with only one book to their credit as well as those who were winners of the Nobel Prize, the Pulitzer Prize or the National Book Award. They heard the works of poets of the past recited by some of our most accomplished actors and actresses: Eva Marie Saint, James Earl Jones, Gregory Peck, Claire Bloom, Princess Grace of Monaco, Michael York, Colleen Dewhurst, George Grizzard, Melvyn Douglas, John Houseman, Brooke Shields, Vanessa Redgrave, Peter Ustinov, Pat Carroll, Jose Ferrer, Zoe Caldwell, Hume Cronyn, Jessica Tandy, Ellen Burstyn, Siobhan McKenna, Richard Kiley, Danny Glover, Julie Harris, Dame Judith Anderson, Jane Alexander, Eli Wallach and Anne Jackson, to name but the most prominent.

In addition to its public programs the Forum maintained a five-county-wide program involving poets who visited high school and middle school classes, thus giving the students their first experience of listening to an author read his own work and then entertain their questions.

The one thing that the Forum did achieve over the period of more than three and a half decades was to make poetry an accepted and expected part of civic life. It also enforced the notion that poetry was ultimately a bardic or oral art, i.e., that poems came into their own finally when they were heard or when they were read as if they were being heard, person to person.

William Butler Yeats wrote that "rhetoric is the language of our fight with others; poetry is the name of our fight with ourselves." Perhaps this is why poetry never addresses itself to masses or the crowd, as is the case with most public discourse, i.e, the language of information called news, the language of advertising, the language of government or the impersonal language of the law or of science. In our era when information is mistaken for wisdom, obscurity for mystery, rudeness for candor, glibness for competence, notoriety for fame, the fouled fonts of language are in need of constant purification and refinement. The late Italo Calvino described this state of affairs and its antidote as follows: "It sometimes seems to me that the pestilence has struck the human race in its most distinctive faculty— that is, the use of words. It is a plague afflicting language, revealing itself in loss of cognition and immediacy, an automatism that tends to level out all expression into the most generic, anonymous and abstract formulas, to dilute meanings, to blunt the edge of expressiveness, extinguishing the spark that shoots out from the collision of words and new circumstances. Literature, and perhaps literature alone can create the anti-bodies to fight this plague of language." Poetry speaks to each of us personally and with absolute sincerity like a private letter, and we nod and assent to the truth of it as we would to the mention of our very names. It places us in a time that is everlastingly now, a time when we go from present to present, a time when we live in that all-too-true-eternity where nothing is ahead and nothing behind but somehow totally alive within us. Everything seems to exist in the present instant, and we breathe that instant as long as the poem has power over us. At times this power is almost too much for us. It transfigures so that we are mysteriously above and beyond history. It makes us more deeply ourselves and more profoundly everybody at the same time.

We live in a time when numerous institutions and their representatives look on man in partial terms. To advertisers he is a consumer. To politicians he is a voter. To television producers he is a viewer. To corporations he is something called personnel. To the military he is a rank. These are all partial views, and they owe a great deal to the influence of technology since technology assumes that all reality—man included—is divisible into parts. This may be true of machines. It is not true of life; divide anything living into its component parts, and it dies in the process. Poetry (and each of the other arts as well) is there to remind us that life comes in wholes, not in fractions. It also helps us to live in what is literally the time being, and it does by simply being what it is. We often confuse the future with expectation. Expectation is closely related to presumption. It's what impels us to want the future to conform to our dream of it. As a matter of fact, the future does not exist at all. We simply presume that it will exist, which means that it exists only within us as a wish. Similarly the past exists within us as our recollections, collective or individual, create it. Factually speaking, the past and future are non-states. Only the present exists, and it is passing even as it happens.

To live in the present is one of the most difficult challenges we face each day, and the arts help us meet this challenge. Unlike children, who live effortlessly in the here and now because they seem to know instinctively that this is all we have, we face the need of having to decide to live in the present. It's not sufficient to realize that all of our appetites live there; something in us always hungers for the illusions of remembering and planning. Hence, we have the need to live right now, to introduce ourselves constantly into the present by making a choice, moral or otherwise. The arts often help us in making these ineluctable choices. And any city, Pittsburgh included, becomes what Rand McNally would call "more livable" to the extent that is welcomes the poets and artists in its midst and heeds their work.

As singular proof of poetry's non-ornamental but organic place in our lives, it is interesting to note that books of poetry, unlike yesterday's newspaper, invariably outlive the poets themselves. This proves that the viability of poetry is not co-terminus with the life of the poet but with the life of the poem, and the life of a genuine poem is dateless. Similarly, the houses and town and cities in which poets were born or where they lived take on an almost sacrosanct identity after the poets have died. Think of Shakespeare and Stratford-on-Avon, or San Francisco-born Robert Frost and his aura in the state of Vermont, or Robinson Jeffers and Big Sur, or Poe in Baltimore, or William Butler Yeats in Sligo and Thoor Ballylee, or Rilke in Muzot, or Jorge Luis Borges in Buenos Aires. This kind of remembrance is reserved for those whose writings have earned them a sacred place not only in the memories of their readers but in those geographical locales that have come to be identified with them. Call it simple reverence or call it a form of idolatry, but it nonetheless exists and attests to the immortality of poetry in both print and in places associated with individual poets.

If poetry and the arts are peripheral and not essential, as some of their detractors insist, why is it that those who seek to impose totalitarian or politically correct strictures (the new totalitarianism of conformity) upon their societies immediately single out poets and artists as enemies of the state and mark them for ridicule, exile or death? The answer is obvious. Poets and artists are those who cannot excuse themselves from expressing what is actually happening in the present. As such they are the natural enemies of all those who would bend others to their manipulative will because they regard people as sheep or simply as multitudes governable only by deception, lies or brute fear. Poetry and the other arts, on the contrary, introduce awe into our lives, and awe is the beginning of the wonder of wisdom, and wisdom returns us to our common humanity. Whatever returns us to our humanity makes us the natural opponents of those who are not beautifiers but uglifiers, who want to take the wonder out of life itself, whose goal is not to enlighten but to dominate. A British poet once wrote that a "poet was someone who comes to terms with his own amazement." And so it is with all the arts. To be amazed, and to be able to amaze others . . . not a bad credential by any standard.

Any city that is respectful of and hospitable to the arts can never be a city that is easily dismissed or ignored. One thinks of Paris and Florence as prime examples. They were not only ennobled by the arts, but they in turn ennobled France and Italy respectively. True, the United States is not yet a nation with the magnanimity and vision of Ireland that offers special tax concessions to writers as a sign of respect as well as an inducement to continued residence. Nor do we honor our most significant writers with ambassadorships as is done in many Latin American countries. But there are cities in the country—and Pittsburgh is one of them—where the arts are not taken for granted and, for differing reasons, supported. And all in all Pittsburgh and cities like it are the better for it.

What is it finally that the arts bring to public life that make their presence indispensable and not merely ornamental? Throughout this book I have stated and shown that Pittsburgh is always in flux. Neighborhoods and landmarks change or are changed, and in turn the changes change or are changed. This leaves us with the sense we are all creatures of history, mere presences in the all-too-brief life of the passing scene. The arts say we are more than that. They speak to us not to remind us of our transience but to confirm us in our common humanity, which somehow allies us with what is everlasting. Having such artistic experiences affords us what Robert Frost defined as a "momentary stay against confusion." And we need such moments if only to offset the feeling that we are mere chips in a millstream. Such affirmations are dateless, and they are as necessary to our lives as love is. Pittsburgh may and certainly will continue to change, but the arts will be there to unite its inhabitants with values that are at once as old and as new as human nature itself.

Vermeer Painting, 1998.

THE AUTHOR

The author of books of poetry, fiction, essays and plays, Samuel Hazo is the director and president of the International Poetry Forum in Pittsburgh, Pennsylvania, where he is also McAnulty Distinguished Professor Emeritus at Duquesne University. His latest books are *Just Once* (poetry), *Spying for God* (essays), *Stills* (fiction), and *Feather* (play). He has been a National Book Award finalist, was chosen the first state poet of the Commonwealth of Pennsylvania in 1993, and received the Maurice English Poetry Award 2003.

THE ARTIST

Robert Qualters has been painting Pittsburgh for thirty years. He has had one-artist shows at the Carnegie Museum of Art and the Pittsburgh Center for the Arts, where he was Artist of the Year in 1985. His work is represented in numerous collections, and he has been awarded multiple public art commissions.

ORDER ADDITIONAL COPIES OF

the Pittsburgh that stays within you

by SAMUEL HAZO
art by Robert Qualters
(ISBN 0-9744715-0-X)

from THE LOCAL HISTORY COMPANY
Publishers of History and Heritage
www.TheLocalHistoryCompany.com
sales@TheLocalHistoryCompany.com

ORDER FORM—PLEASE PRINT CLEARLY

NAME _____

COMPANY (if applicable) _____

ADDRESS _____

CITY _____ STATE _____ ZIP _____

PHONE _____ PLEASE include your phone number so we can contact you in case there is a problem with your order.

Please allow 2-4 weeks for delivery. Prices are subject to change without notice. All book sales are final. US shipments only (contact us for information on international orders). Payable by check, money order, or Discover/Visa/MC in US funds (no cash orders accepted).

PLEASE SEND _____ copies at $21.95 each .... Subtotal: $_____

Sales Tax: PA residents (outside Allegheny County) add 6% per copy

Allegheny County, PA residents add 7% per copy $_____

Add $5 shipping/packaging for the first copy and $1 each additional copy $_____

TOTAL AMOUNT DUE: $_____

PAYMENT BY CHECK/MONEY ORDER:

____   Enclosed is my check/money order made payable to *The Local History Company* for the total amount due above.

PAYMENT BY VISA or MASTERCARD:

Bill my _____ Visa _____ MasterCard   Account # _____

(Address above must be the same as on file with your credit card company)

Expires _____   Name as it appears on your card _____

Signature _____

Mail or Fax your order to: **The Local History Company**
(Fax 412-362-8192)   112 NORTH Woodland Road
Pittsburgh, PA 15232
Or—Call 412-362-2294 with your order.

QUANTITY ORDERS INVITED

*This and other books from **The Local History Company** are available at special quantity discounts for bulk purchases or sales promotions, premiums, fund raising, or educational use by corporations, institutions, and other organizations. Special imprints, messages, and excerpts can also be produced to meet your specific needs.*

For details, please write or telephone:

*Special Sales, **The Local History Company***
112 NORTH Woodland Road, Pittsburgh, PA 15232-2849, 412-362-2294.
Please specify how you intend to use the books (promotion, resale, fund raising, etc.)